PILGRIMAGE OF A PROSELYTE:
From Auschwitz to Jerusalem

BOOKS BY DAVID PATTERSON

Faith and Philosophy, 1982
The Affirming Flame: Religion, Language, Literature,
    1988
*Literature and Spirit: Essays on Bakhtin and His
    Contemporaries,* 1988
In Dialogue and Dilemma with Elie Wiesel, 1991
*The Shriek of Silence: A Phenomenology of the
    Holocaust Novel,* 1992

Translations

Confession, by Leo Tolstoy, 1983
Diary of a Superfluous Man, by Ivan Turgenev, 1983
The Forged Coupon, by Leo Tolstoy, 1984
Winter Notes on Summer Impressions,
    by Fyodor Dostoevsky, 1988
The Gospel According to Tolstoy, by Leo Tolstoy, 1992

PILGRIMAGE OF A PROSELYTE:
From Auschwitz to Jerusalem

by

David Patterson

 Jonathan David Publishers, Inc.
Middle Village, New York 11379

PILGRIMAGE OF A PROSELYTE:
From Auschwitz to Jerusalem

Copyright ©1993

by

David Patterson

Jonathan David Publishers, Inc.
68-22 Eliot Avenue
Middle Village, NY 11379

1994 1996 1997 1995 1993
2 4 6 8 10 9 7 5 3 1

Library of Congress Cataloging-in-Publication Data

Patterson, David, 1948–
  Pilgrimage of a proselyte: from Auschwitz to Jerusalem/David Patterson.
    p. cm.
  Includes index.
  ISBN 0-8246-0363-X
  1. Patterson, David, 1948- . 2. Proselyte and proselyting,
Jewish—Converts from Christianity. 3. Holocaust, Jewish (1939-
1945)—Influence. 4. Patterson, David, 1948—Journeys.
I. Title.
Bm729.P7P3 1993
296.7'1—dc20
[B]   93-13626
                                                              CIP

Book design by Jennifer Vignone
Printed in the United States of America

**For the Ashes
and for Eliyah**

Preface

IN ORDER TO PROVIDE an autobiographical context for the pilgrimage that took me from Auschwitz to Jerusalem, I should say a word or two about my life prior to my conversion to Judaism. Born in 1948, I was brought up as a Methodist. While my paternal grandparents were quite religious, my parents were less so. But I did attend church, at times sporadically, at times regularly. During my pre-teen years I lived in the belief that Jesus heard my every prayer and that he took my prayers right to the ear of God. By the time I was eight years old I was reading the Bible weekly and checking out books about biblical figures from the library. I remember being especially taken by the brief story of Enoch, who was taken by God without having to suffer the sting of death (Genesis 5:24). It must be nice not to have to die, I thought. Perhaps if I am good enough God will take me too, and I won't have to die.

For a time being good enough meant being Christian enough. And so my study of the Bible in general and of the Gospels in particular continued until I was about sixteen. At that point what I had seen of the laws of nature, which necessitated the death of all, struck me as more compelling than the power of faith. Thus an interest in science began to displace my concern with Jesus. Instead of Matthew, Mark, and Luke, I was reading Einstein, Bohr, and Eddington. Although I still wanted to believe in Jesus (what that meant, exactly, I did not know), I was unable to grasp the Christian view of how the world is arranged, how death is destroyed, or how one man takes the place of all the rest in an expiation of sins. In science I thought I had found something that at least made sense; the formulas explained it all. When I set off for college two years later, I became a physics major with the goal of becoming a nuclear physicist.

After two years of college physics, however, I began to understand why Robert Oppenheimer described the early years of quantum mechanics not only as a time of excitement but as a time of terror. For me, the terror lay in the fact that physics placed a measure of power in hands that did not hold a proportionate measure of wisdom. Feeling that the world was in much greater need of humanitarian insight than technological advance, I took up a study of philosophy. In those days my religious life was nonexistent. I was too smart, too logical, for such things. The endeavor overtaken by science was now eclipsed by social activism informed by rationalism. When I was not studying existential philosophy, I was involved in civil rights and anti-war activities. People do not need prayers, I maintained, but a helping hand. I tried to act as though all depended on me, but I did not know how to pray as if all depended on God.

Then I discovered Soren Kierkegaard, the eminent Christian thinker of nineteenth-century Denmark, and with that discovery I returned to an effort to embrace Christianity. Faith, he helped me to realize, is not a second-rate form of knowledge that we settle for when reason fails to work; rather it is a passion, a way of being, steeped in a Paradox that is the pathway to truth. I wanted to seek the faith that was a necessary basis for the sanctity of human life, that was the force of life itself. This renewed religious concern took my studies in yet another direction, to literature in general and to Russian literature in particular. By the time I graduated with a degree in philosophy, I was convinced that literary texts were able to address religious questions on a level more profound than in most philosophical texts.

With this conviction and striving for Christian conviction, I pursued a program of graduate study in comparative literature. Now married to a woman who was reared as a Baptist, I continued to study Christian texts, both in philosophy and in literature. Among the literary figures who influenced me most during those years were Pascal, Blake, Dostoevsky, and Tolstoy. By 1978, when I completed a doctoral dissertation on literary and philosophical expressions of faith, I had also studied Tertullian, Augustine, Aquinas, Luther, and other Christian thinkers. Still subscribing to the existential view that doing has an impact on being and that human relation is linked to divine relation, I moved on to an examination of Martin Buber. Through him I was first introduced to a body of thought that presented itself as explicitly Jewish: the tales of the Hasidim. I soon developed a genuine love for the Hasidic masters and came to regard them as my teachers.

Buber was the one Jewish thinker to appear on the reading list for a seminar on literary philosophy that I taught in my first university appointment. My students often came to see me to talk about the ideas in the books we were reading, and I was in the habit of recommending to them additional texts according to their concerns. To one I would offer a bit of Dostoevsky, to another Camus, and Nietzsche to a third. Then one day a young man from one of my classes knocked on my office door. In his hand he held a thin paperback volume with a wrinkled binding.

"Here," he said, placing the book on my desk. "You've had me read several books, so I brought one for you to read."

I glanced at the book's cover: it was *Night* by Elie Wiesel.

That evening, after rocking to sleep my new baby girl, I began reading the book placed in my hands like a message borne from another shore. I devoured every page, and every page consumed me. This book led me to Wiesel's *Dawn*, then *The Accident*, then *The Town Beyond the Wall*, on and on, until I had read everything I could find that had come from the hand and soul of Elie Wiesel. I felt that in this man I had encountered a witness who had made me into a witness. Once confronted with his tales and his testimony from Planet Auschwitz, I was myself called to the stand. It was a summons that I could not refuse, a responsibility that I had to bear if I was to be a human being. But his books contained words that were unfamiliar to me, such as Pesach and Yom Kippur, Midrash and Zohar. And so, in order to meet my responsibility to and for all that is precious in human life, I knew that I had to find out what these terms meant.

Although I continued to think of myself as a Christian, I was now reading texts about Judaism. Indeed, having begun a study of the Holocaust through my study of Wiesel, I felt that it was my duty as a Christian to examine this life that was nearly wiped out in the heart of Christendom. The more I learned of Jewish history, the more aghast I was at the suffering that the Jews have endured at the hands of Christians. I learned of the trail of blood left in the wake of the Crusaders as they passed through the Rhineland in 1096; the institution of the Jew Badge initiated by Innocent III in 1215; the Rindfleisch massacres in Germany in 1298; the expulsions of the Jews from Spain in 1391 and 1492; the Chmielnitzki slaughter that lasted from 1648 to 1658; the terrible years of the Russian pogroms after 1881. Those whose sins had been washed clean by the Blood of the Lamb seemed to thrive on the blood of the Jews. And then there was the Holocaust, the Shoah, the Hurban, the Six Million (or more), the million and a half children, the synagogues filled and set aflame, the Slaughter of Innocents burned alive, the Muselmaenner, murder after murder, beyond the limits of mind and imagination—all of it carried out if not by the hands then with the complicity of baptized Christians in lands where Christian civilization was most triumphant.

And I too thought of myself as a Christian.

At first—and for years—I tried to convince myself that there was no pattern here, that the atrocities so often committed by Christians in the name of Christianity were not the work of true Christians. According to Christian teaching, God is love, and we must love our enemies, not kill them (as though the Jews might be regarded as the enemies of the Christians!). Did the Nazis not throw some Christians into the camps as well? Well, yes. But not because they were Christians. But didn't some Christians, the Righteous among the Nations, actually help the Jews at the risk of their own lives? Yes. Some. But not most. Not enough. Jesus teaches us in Matthew 7:18 that a good tree cannot bear evil fruit. If we are to believe him, then what are we to say about all this fruit that announces the infinity of evil, this fruit grown in the soil of Christendom?

I could not get past this difficulty. According to orthodox Christianity, the only path to God leads through the Christ. Those who embrace this path, though they lie on their death bed, are saved from damnation. Those who refuse this path, regardless of their age, are unredeemed. Therefore, I once heard a Baptist preacher declare, if Adolf Eichmann should repent his sins on his way to the gallows and accept Jesus, he is saved; but the children he sent to the gas chambers have gone from the fires of the crematoria to the fires of hell. This seemed to me to be the logical outcome of the teaching that the New Testament supersedes the Old Testament, that the Covenant between God and Abraham has been taken over by a New Covenant. If the children of Abraham must now find their way into heaven by joining the followers of Jesus, then the Jews themselves are superseded. And, as long as they persist in their stiff-necked denial of the Savior, they are damned. Logical, all too logical. And, if history is proof of anything, it seemed to be Christian, all too Christian.

The more I thought about this supersessionist basis of Christianity, the more I had trouble with other difficulties. Was Jesus, in fact, the one whose coming was foretold and awaited by the prophets? Seeking an answer to this question, I turned to the books of the prophets, and, as far as the Nazarene was concerned, I found more discrepancy than correspondence. Where, for example, was the ingathering of the Jews prophesied by Isaiah (27:12) or the inscription of the Law of the Holy One upon the hearts of all nations, as Jeremiah foretold (31:33)? Nor did I find among the prophets any indication that the Messiah was to be the incarnation of God Himself or that he would purify the world of its sins by being crucified and then resurrected. I began to wonder whether the second-century Christian heretic Marcion was right after all: Christianity has no essential connection with Judaism. For a time, however, I suspended these thoughts under the assumption that I might be wrong about the prophets and that my own shortcomings had resulted in a misreading of those texts.

By 1988 I had spent ten years wrestling with all of these questions about Christianity, and I continued my pursuit of Holocaust studies. During the last four or five of those years I regularly attended Quaker meetings, hoping that there I might find a version of Christianity that would make murder—even the murder of a "superseded" people—impossible. For a time, I was satisfied with my life as a would-be Quaker, or so I thought. In the meantime, I was divorced in 1985, and two years later I married a Jewish woman. When we were married in the spring of 1987 I indicated to her that I had no intention of converting, but that I had no objection to raising our children in a Jewish household. This was enough for her to agree to the inter-marriage, and she never pressured me to consider conversion. It came to pass that in January 1988 a little girl was born to us.

Upon my marriage to my second wife, I came into a "dowry" of nearly three thousand books on Jewish religion and on the Holocaust. From the time I met my wife in 1986, even unto this day, most of my study has been tied to these texts. In 1987 I began writing a book on the "Holocaust novel," and in the summer of that year I participated in the international Holocaust conference "Remembering for the Future" held in Oxford and London. Attended by hundreds of Christian and Jewish scholars from all over the world, the conference gave me the opportunity to speak with dozens of people about the questions that haunted me for so long. One thing I realized from these talks was that if the Nazis were not to be allowed a victory after the fact, then Jewish life, Jewish religion, and Jewish tradition had to be recovered and nurtured. Given what I had understood to be the truth of that life and tradition, I felt that I had to be part of the religion. And so upon my return to the United States I contacted a rabbi about converting to Judaism.

What led to this decision, I think, was not a Christian's feelings of guilt over the suffering Christians had caused the Jews for centuries. It was not something that could be reduced to saying No to the Nazis or to a flight from what I may have regarded as a false doctrine. I prefer to regard it, rather, as a pursuit of a divine and human truth. Thankfully, my decision to convert did not cause my parents or anyone else among my Christian relatives any serious concern. During my year and a half of study with the rabbi they were quite supportive, happy for the unity that it had brought to my family and home life. In the section that follows, "Before the Pilgrimage," I say more about this transformation.

Before the Pilgrimage

On the 13th of Tevet 5750 (early January 1990) I became a Jew. Or perhaps it would be better to say that I stepped across a threshold leading to the path toward becoming a Jew. As Edmond Jabès* has pointed out, a Jew is one who is continually "just on the point of becoming Jewish...The affirmation 'I am Jewish' is already a regression, a stop, a way of falling asleep in that condition." And to fall asleep in that condition is to slip out of the Jewish condition.

If it is nothing else, the Jewish condition is a condition of wakefulness, a condition of perpetual motion and interrogation of God, the world, and above all oneself. Even a Jew, then, must become Jewish. To be a Jew is to be engaged in the process of becoming Jewish, of eternally becoming more—more responsible, more thankful, more generous, more loving. And so on the 13th of Tevet 5750, longing to become more by becoming other, I sat before a *Bet Din*** convened by Rabbi Charles Shalman of the

---

*Edmond Jabès (1912-1991), French novelist, poet, and thinker, born in Cairo and emigrated to France just after World War II.
**A council of three men who pronounce judgment on points of Jewish ritual and Jewish law.

Emanuel Synagogue in Oklahoma City. I underwent the ritual circumcision and the immersion in the *mikvah*.* And from those waters of purification I emerged transformed, body and soul.

It is one of the great mysteries of the faith that the proselyte takes on not only the spiritual being of the Chosen but their physical essence as well, like a branch grafted onto a tree that receives the sap rising up from the roots. I am reminded of the summer of 1989, when I was in Israel doing some research on novels written in response to the Holocaust. During my stay at Hebrew University, on July 6, an Arab terrorist forced Bus 405 over the side of a cliff along the highway from Tel-Aviv to Jerusalem. The entire country came to a halt. It was as if some part of a single body had been struck and wounded when the Jews on that bus were killed.

And a strange thing happened to me, which now does not seem so strange. Upon hearing the news, even before I could make out all the details broadcast in Hebrew, I had the *physical* sensation of something cutting into me, of something like a wound arising from within my own body. The thought that came with it was not "they have killed them" but "they have killed us." At the time I tried to dismiss such a notion as lunacy, but it would not go away. Now I realize that the Jewish transformation I was undergoing was taking on a visceral form: I was becoming Jewish *in body*.

After I had met with the Bet Din and had risen transformed from the waters of the *mikvah,* an elderly man, a pious man, who sat on the Bet Din said something to me in his East European accent: "I hope you understand, Avraham David ben Avraham, that now you have tied your fate to the fate and the memory of the Six Million."

"Yes, Mr. Slutzky," I assured him. "I understand. And I won't forget."

---

*A bath used for various rites of cleansing and purification.

But, of course, I did not understand. Despite years of wrestling with a memory that was not my own, despite decades of breathing the air and eating the bread that harbors the ashes of the dead, I did not understand. I pray that I shall never forget, but I know that I shall never understand. I have been occupied, even preoccupied, with the Six Million for a long time. Indeed, when I sat before the Bet Din, I had the unshakable feeling that I sat before those silent eyes as well.

But the truth of the Six Million, the truth to which and for which I must forever answer, is a truth that I shall never know, one that remains hidden in the ashes, awaiting with us all the coming of the Messiah. Perhaps, like His holy name, their truth is among those things that preceded the Creation. I have returned now from a journey that led me to those ashes. I have stood on the edge of that truth. But it recedes even as I approach it. And so it remains just beyond my reach, inviolate, silently calling my name.

A large part of the forces that moved me to come before the Bet Din lay in that summons. During the year and a half that I spent studying with Rabbi Shalman he tried at least three times to dissuade me, in keeping with the tradition that dates back to the story of Ruth and Naomi. I remember that the first date scheduled for my meeting with the Bet Din turned out to be a day when there were some difficulties with the mikvah. The encounter, therefore, had to be postponed.

The Rabbi felt that perhaps I should spend the meantime writing down all the whys and wherefores behind my decision to convert. Knowing that nothing happens by chance (*chance* is not a kosher word, as one of I. B. Singer's characters once put it), I agreed that this was a needful part of the process, that this too was part of the decision handed down by the Bet Din. This assignment would situate my own soul among those judges. And, in response to the assignation of my soul, I wrote the following:

"A character in Elie Wiesel's novel *The Oath* raises a question about the perilous nature of the Jewish condition in the world. 'Who could be so stupid,' he asks, 'as to envy our lot?' I read this line some ten years ago, and somewhere inside of me a silent voice—silenced, perhaps, by myself—answered, 'I am, God help me. I am so stupid.'

"At that time I was, as I still am, a student of philosophy and literature, but my interest in these areas has always been more religious or spiritual than academic. In my books and articles I constantly struggle to make the movement from academic curiosity to human accountability. If my labor over my texts does not transform itself into a deeper embrace of my wife and children, then it is the worst of vanities. Life's attachment to life, the word's link to meaning, one human being's relation to another, the human relation to God—this is what I try to place at the core of my relation to philosophy and literature. I struggle, though not always successfully, to make the student in me into a human being. I labor to make my studies into a labor of love.

"In my studies of Elie Wiesel [which led to my current study of the Shoah] I read another line that brought me a step closer to this path I have chosen. 'There are times,' he writes in *A Beggar in Jerusalem,* 'when one must assume the Jewish condition in order to remain human.' The Shoah divided people into two categories: victims and executioners. Realizing this, I heard a question put to me, a question that arose from within me and from beyond me: Where are you?

"It is not enough to answer, *'Hineni,* Here I am,' and leave it at that. The first proselyte, Abraham, answers twice when he is called because, Rabbi Adin Steinsaltz once told me, the response generates the need and the capacity to respond again. And so the responsibility grows ever deeper. A trace of the Infinite opens up in the human being, and the debt increases in the measure that it is paid. Since, for me, the question was born from the categories inherited from the Shoah, it also arose from a question raised by Emmanuel Levinas.* The concern for existence, he argues, does not lie in the question of why there is something rather than nothing, as Heidegger and Leibnitz before him supposed. No, the question is this: do I live by killing? Unlike some Christians and Moslems, over the centuries the Jews have generally refused to live by killing.

"Another thing, an important thing, that turned me away from the Christian religion in which I was reared lies in the distinction between the human and the divine, which is essential to the distinction between good and evil, light and darkness, the holy and the profane. No one who is born of a woman—not even Jesus, especially not Jesus—is God.

"To insist that Jesus alone is divine, excluding the spark of the divine in the rest of humanity, is to renounce both God and humanity. Also, I do not see how the words of the prophets who foretold the coming of the Messiah could possibly be made to describe the coming of Jesus and the events surrounding his life. There was no ingathering of the Jews, for example, and there is little indication that the Law of the Holy One, blessed be He, has been inscribed upon the hearts of all people.

"Many of the teachings of Jesus, however, still mean a great deal to me, as do the teachings of other Jews, such as Judah Halevi,** Maimonides,† the Baal Shem Tov,†† Franz

---

*French phenomenologist, born in Kovno, Lithuania, 1906.

**Jewish thinker and poet, author of the *Kuzari*, born in Toledo, ca. 1085, died in the Holy Land, 1140.

†Rabbi Moshe ben Maimon, or Rambam (1135-1204), author of *The Guide for the Perplexed* and the greatest of the Jewish medieval philosophers.

††Literally, "The Good Master of the Name," he is Israel ben Eliezer (1700-1760), founder of Hasidism.

Rosenzweig,* and Elie Wiesel. Am I rejecting the religion of Jesus in my choosing to become Jewish? Not exactly. I am rejecting the religion of Paul, Augustine, Aquinas, and Luther for the religion of Abraham, Isaac, Jacob, and Moses, which, of course, is the religion of Jesus.

"In *The Last of the Just* André Schwartz-Bart describes Jesus as a misunderstood Hasid. Perhaps it was my 'Christian' inclination that made Hasidism so attractive to me, for my study of Hasidism was another step along the way that has brought me to Judaism. It seems to me that at least the initial 'Christian' message was the same as what Martin Buber claims is the Hasidic message: love more. *The Shma*** summons us to hear the Voice, and the first thing the Voice tells us to do is to love—love God and show that love by loving one another, by loving God's creation and God's law, *bechol-me'odechah*, with all the more that we have within us.

"The Ten Commandments, the Ten Utterances, are divided into two realms of relation: *adam l'adam,* the relation of man to man, and *adam la-Makom,* the relation of man to the Place, that is, of man to God. Yet both of these constitute a single relation, just as God constitutes a single Presence. This is what the *mitzvot,* the commandments, that are grounded in the Ten Utterances are all about: seeing, hearing, feeling, knowing that the path to the Holy One and the portals through which He enters life lead through what there is to love in human life. You want to show God your love for Him? Then embrace the human being who stands before you.

"This is what Judaism is about. This is why I have chosen to become a Jew. In Christianity we see what happens

---

*German Jew (1886-1929), author of *The Star of Redemption,* known for his revival of Judaism.

**First word in the prayer that begins, "Hear, O Israel, the Lord our God, the Lord is One" (Deuteronomy 6:4), recited at least twice daily by religious Jews.

when the *mitzvot* are lost; in Islam we see what happens when love is lost. I choose Judaism because that is where the *mitzvot* and love are interwoven: hear and love, with body and soul. For each needs the other in order to live, just as each person needs his neighbor.

"I say I have chosen Judaism, but in a way it has chosen me. I say I want to become a Jew, but in a way I *must* become a Jew. I cannot do otherwise and remain a human being. And in this *cannot* I find a genuine freedom, at once choosing and being chosen. For freedom lies not in doing whatever you want to do but in realizing what you must do. Thus freedom and destiny are promised to each other: to be free is to have a mission, a message, a testimony to bear.

"The question has been put to me: Where are you? And I must struggle to answer, *'Hineni,'* with my words, my deeds, and my life, making my life into an affirmation not only of what is ethical but of what is holy, of what there is to love. In *The Thirteen Petalled Rose* Rabbi Steinsaltz describes repentance, *teshuvah,* as a type of conversion. For me, conversion is a kind of repentance, a repentance for not having been what I am, for not choosing as I have been chosen. Why Judaism? Because it is *HaShem* (the Name) who puts the question and thus chooses the one who is questioned.

"'But,' I will be asked, 'how do you know?'

"And I answer: the Voice tells me so. The Silence tells me so. The ashes tell me so.

"Why Judaism? Because there Silence is not the deaf and mute silence of nothingness but a mode of speaking adopted by the Infinite, by the *En Sof.* There a man can argue with God and embrace God in his argument, making the question he puts to God into a question about himself and his relation to God—making the question itself part of God. In Hebrew the word for question is *she' elah.* In the midst of that word we have the *alef lamed,* the *el,* of

God's name: God is part of the fabric of the question itself.

"And so I am constantly thrown back to the issue of hearing and response, of loving and choosing, realizing that in this, in the questions we raise and answer, we are chosen from the womb, chosen by the Good before we have ever given the slightest thought to choosing. We can choose whether to testify or to remain silent, but we cannot choose whether or not we have been summoned.

"Which brings me to another point. I have wondered whether conversion was even possible. After all, having a Jewish mother, I thought, was a requirement for being a Jew. But I realized that to reduce Judaism to this would be to make it into gross materialism. To be born of a Jewish mother is enough to make a person a Jew not because of the blood alone but because of the Voice that cries out from the blood. It is not the flesh alone but the linkage between the flesh and the spirit that makes a person born of a Jewish mother a Jew. And the establishment of this linkage between the spiritual and the material is what makes conversion possible.

"In the Talmud we are told that everyone who is a Jew has three defining characteristics: modesty, generosity, and lovingkindness. There is a story, in fact, about a man during the time of the Babylonian Exile who was in need of help. He was told that there was a Jewish community living in Babylon and that there he could find help. But he entered the community only to have doors closed in his face and no helping hand extended to him. And he concluded that he had been misinformed, that this was a renegade community passing itself off as Jewish. Cervantes has said that virtue ennobles the blood, not the other way around. Being Jewish has something like that about it. Just as the blood brings responsibility, so does taking on responsibility transform the blood.

"Thus in my conversion I shall bleed. I shall offer up my blood, and it will take on new substance. Blood offered is blood transformed. Blood transformed is life transfigured. The spirit enters the body and merges with it when the body bleeds in sacrifice. It enters through the wound.

"What about study? Isn't it necessary to know something if you are to become a Jew? I once thought that I had to know everything. But I see now that studying is more important than knowing. For a Jew, study is a form of prayer, and so it has always been for me. As a Sage once put it, when I pray I speak to God; when I study God speaks to me. For whatever it is worth, it is in my nature to study, and I have been blessed enough to make a living at it, as well as to try to make a life of it. Deciding something about the texts that I encounter, I am faced with deciding something about my own life; I become a witness in my response to the word, as I struggle to join life and word in the act of response. This is another feature of Judaism that has drawn me into it.

"It is all too true that I do not know enough, that I do not understand enough. And yet the words of a Hasidic Rabbi, Naphtali of Ropshitz (1759-1826), come to me: God does not ask that you understand the Torah, only that you study it. Thus the Talmud begins with page two in order to remind us that no matter how many times we have been through it, we have not even begun. It reminds me of an exchange between Ivan and Alyosha Karamazov in Dostoevsky's novel *The Brothers Karamazov.* 'Am I to love life without knowing the meaning of it?' Ivan asks. And Alyosha answers, 'You must love life without understanding the meaning of it, for that is the only way you can ever hope to understand its meaning.'

"What is said of life here applies to Jewish life. You don't understand it? Love it, live it, and then you will understand. Why do we wear *talit* and *tefillin,* the prayer shawl and phylacteries? Don them, and you will begin to know. I have studied the Yom Kippur service, but this year, when I went through the rites and rituals of atonement, I understood far more than ever before. It was as though I had had a brush with death and was given a second chance, as though I were resurrected when I should have died. I realized, for instance, that the Yizkor memorial service was not separate from the rites of atonement but essential to those rites, not something we take time out for but an act of remembrance definitively linked to the process of redemption. And, in *living* this, I understood a bit more about the Baal Shem's statement that just as oblivion is tied to exile, so is memory at the root of redemption.

"If my conversion entails a movement of return, it also includes a process of remembrance. In all the world there is but a single place where a great treasure is hidden, and that place is the spot where you are standing. With Jewish eyes I behold the treasure, the thing very nigh unto me, to which I have been blind. Remembrance transforms vision and sanctifies what we see; thus we are summoned to *zachor v'shamor,* to remember and observe. This is the function of every *mitzvah.* The *mitzvot* sanctify, and sanctification breeds revelation. With Jewish eyes I see more of what Buber had in mind when he said that the thundering revelations on which the great religions are founded are essentially the same as the quiet one that happens everywhere all around us. It is with Jewish ears that I listen to hear the *kol demamah dakah,* the thin Voice of Silence. Hearing this, how can I not become a Jew? I have no choice. Or rather, I choose to have no choice.

"Not long ago something happened to me when my wife Gerri lit the Sabbath candles, something that has never happened before, something that told me I was becoming a Jew. For an instant I sensed the *olam ha-emet,* the World of Truth, entering the moment at hand, the eternal creeping into time; for a second I had an inkling of what must be remembered and observed, *zachor v'shamor,* remembered and protected, nurtured, cared for. I held back my tears, though they were tears of joy, for fear of embarrassing my children. For an instant moving into the Sabbath was like crossing a threshold into heaven, leaving behind the things and the activities, all the gravities, of this world. I was not only entering the Sabbath, but the Sabbath was entering me. I think it was the Jew I am becoming that saw this, felt this, in the Sabbath. And I understood what Rabbi Abraham Joshua Heschel (1909-1972) meant when he said that what we are lies in what the Sabbath means to us. Such an understanding is not so much a reason for being attracted to Judaism as a reason for *having* to be Jewish.

"I have been told, 'You don't have to become Jewish to study Jewish philosophy, religion, literature, and so on.' But if, as I believe, this is where the truth lies, then in order to study Jewish thought, Jewish spirituality, and Judaism, then I must be Jewish: I must become one with what I study, if what I study is truth.

"Rabbi Heschel once pointed out that one thing which the Kotzker* and Kierkegaard had in common was this: both understood that truth is not something we know but something we are, or are in the process of becoming. Studying the truth of Judaism, struggling to understand or at least respond to this truth, I must become the truth of Judaism. And in order to do that, I must become a Jew. To be the truth is to live the truth as best one can. To study Judaism, in this sense, is to become a Jew, living in the observance of as many *mitzvot* as one possibly can. This means that conversion is not only a closure but an opening; to convert is not to complete a task but to undertake a task that has no completion.

"Does this mean that the Torah and I are one and the same? No. But it does mean that I must join the Torah to my life and my life to the Torah, if I am to have any hope of living in the truth that engenders what there is to love in life. That is what underlies the prayer, 'Grant us a por-

---

*Menachem Mendel of Kotzk (1787-1859), Hasidic rabbi.

tion in Thy Torah.' That is why the Torah is known as the *ets-chaim*, as the Tree of Life. Hence, for me, becoming a Jew is a matter of life and death. As it is written in the Midrash,* there are those who are dead before they die. Right now I am struggling for life, laboring to be born out of the womb of the Word. As I see it, therefore, I must become a Jew if I am to study the Torah. For to study the truth of the Torah is to endeavor to become that truth through an act of response, a response which is a *teshuvah.*

"I have been told, 'You don't have to become a Jew in order to have a place in the *olam-ha-ba,* in the World to Come. Be an upright, ethical man, and this will be enough.' God knows that being an upright, ethical man is no small achievement. But that is just the point: God knows. Once I have realized this—once I have recognized that in creation there is revelation—then redemption becomes an issue that cannot be abrogated. And redemption cannot be won by ethics alone.

"When the question of redemption arises, then with the matter of the ethical comes the matter of the holy. With the relation of *adam l'adam* comes the relation of *adam la-Makom;* with the man comes the Jew—once I have realized that being a man entails not only the human-to-human relation but the human-to-God relation as well. Ethics can prescribe behavior, but it cannot engender love. Being Jewish and observing the *mitzvot* involves not only a certain mode of behavior but a certain mode of being; it centers not only on what is *musari,* or moral, but on what is *kadosh,* on what is holy. In Judaism—and I think only in Judaism—these two are combined. To remember and observe the *mitzvot* is to join the ethical with the holy.

"The *mitzvot* with which the Holy One blesses His children are not merely rules for behavior; far more than that,

---

*A word that means "seeking" or "searching," Midrash designates a collection of tales and commentary on biblical texts compiled from approximately the fifth through the thirteenth centuries.

they are portals through which all that is holy enters life and sanctifies life, joining life to life. If a human being is to meet his responsibility of sanctifying life, then he too must become such a portal, and, for me, this means becoming a Jew. If I am to live a life that sanctifies life, then I must observe and protect the *mitzvot* of the Jews *as a Jew,* not from the outside but from within, so that Within and Above, Above and Between, become synonyms.

"God knows that being an ethical, upright man is difficult enough. But because God knows, this is not enough. To be a good man, chosen by the Good even before we choose, is to love *bechol-me'odechah,* with all the 'mores.' Through the 'mores' the holy enters life, and life is *Life* only as the holy enters into it, cuts through it, and transforms it. Knowing this, how can I *not* become a Jew?

"I have been told, 'You're crazy. Why take upon yourself all the *tsoris,* all the misery of being a Jew? It's so much easier if you don't have to be a Jew.' Yes, from a certain standpoint I am crazy; from a certain standpoint it is much easier. But, as the Baal Shem Tov once said, when the deaf see people dancing, they take them for madmen. Like it or not, I hear the music, and I have to dance, dance or die, and die in my dancing.

"For me, to be a Jew is a matter of life *and* death. As much as I long to live as a Jew, I see that I must die as a Jew. When Rabbi Akiba was being tortured to death by the Romans in 135 C.E., he sang his praise to God, because now, he said, he could love God with all his heart, all his soul, and all the 'mores.' Rabbi Steinsaltz told me that some people prefer a warm, comfortable bed to lie in, while others see that they have a mountain to climb. Faced with the mountain, we are faced with the task of making not only life but also death into an achievement, of making death into a testimony to the holiness of life, into a *Kiddush HaShem.* 'Each time one man dies on his feet,' Elie Wiesel puts it in *The Town Beyond the Wall,* 'another man is saved.'

"The last time I was in Israel it struck me that I could be killed for being a Jew. The idea frightened me. But it also occurred to me that to be killed for being a Jew meant being killed for living within the relationships that sanctify life. Knowing I must die, I know I must make my death into a testimony, if my life is to have any meaning or substance. Why a Jewish death? For all the reasons underlying a Jewish life. The Jewish death is a sanctification of life, a portal through which the holy enters into life. I must live as a Jew, therefore, because I must die as a Jew. The *Kaddish* is not just a prayer for the dead; it is a prayer said by the living who must engage in the *act,* in the task, of dying. The Jewish death, like the Jewish life, is a sanctification of the Holy Name and therefore of life itself. And so I must live *and* die as a Jew. I take upon myself the *tsoris* and the misery of being a Jew because I know that there is something worse than this misery, something worse than death itself.

"So you see, I cannot study Judaism without becoming a Jew. It is not enough for me to be an ethical man, however difficult that may be. And the misery and the danger of being a Jew, as well as all the joy and thanksgiving that it brings, make it all the more needful that I become a Jew. I can refuse the choice, but I cannot relinquish the responsibility. And in order to assume the responsibility, I must assume a portion of the vulnerability—as a Jew.

"Without this vulnerability, even unto death, there is no life, no truth, no holiness. And it is precisely this vulnerability that transforms the 'for me' into the 'for the other' of responsibility. I must become a Jew for the sake of the other—for my wife, my children, my parents, my brothers, my friends, my students, my community. Only by way of this 'for the other' does anything that is for myself take on meaning.

"It seems to me that this linkage between vulnerability and responsibility is distinctively Jewish, and it is as a Jew that I must establish the linkage in my life. A Jew is chosen not for privilege but for responsibility, for testimony, not only to be a light but to transform darkness into light. The Jewish people are not only the chosen people; having been chosen, they must become the choosing people. Choosing life, responding to suffering, bearing witness to the holy—all of this and more constitutes the task of being a light unto the nations. To the extent that I have seen the light, I must become the light. A person cannot receive the revelation without taking on the responsibility of becoming part of it, without becoming a messenger who is himself the message. Such is the project of redemption.

"The light that has been offered to me comes from Sinai; the darkness to which and for which I must answer comes from Auschwitz. The one comes from the flames of the God who is a consuming fire, the other from the flames of mothers, fathers, and children consumed by fire. If I am to receive the light that is a Jewish light, the light that transforms darkness into light, then I must offer up that light *as a Jew*. If I am not a Jewish witness, then I do not offer the life I have received, and therefore I lose that life. If I am not a Jewish witness, then I have not answered as I have been called, and therefore I lose the One who has summoned me. Losing Him, I lose my wife and children, family and friends, students and community—everything. Losing Him, I am among those who are dead before they die. And that places me in the category of executioners."

And so, having written down these reflections, I came before the Bet Din on the 13th of Tevet 5750. About a year and a half later, on the 28th of Iyar 5751 (May 12, 1991), I continued along the path I had taken up at Emanuel Synagogue and set out on a journey that led me from the Kingdom of Night to the Land of the Covenant.

For several months I had been considering writing a book on Holocaust memoirs, one that would pursue the relation between memory and redemption. Such texts, it seemed to me, constitute more than mere recollections of the past; they are part of a needful movement of return, part of that *teshuvah* that alone opens up a future. Although I had been engaged in Holocaust studies for many years, I had been to only one concentration camp site, to Dachau. This new research project seemed to be the perfect occasion to make a trip to the sites of some of the death camps in Poland and from there to go on to the Hebrew University Library in Jerusalem. And because it was a research project, I decided to take a notebook and record the encounters of each day.

But the trip turned out to be much more than I had anticipated. And the notes I took proved to be something other than bits of information about a topic for a book. The things we seek and the words we utter are always much more than we think they are. At first I was not aware of it, but the journey soon proved to be more of a pilgrimage than a research trip, one that was essential to my being as a proselyte, to my essence as a Jew. And the writing that I did along the way, the words I committed to paper, proved to be a critical part of hearing some shred of the voices that spoke to me from within and from beyond the silence that shrouds them. Having chosen this way of the chosen, I soon realized that the path leading into my soul now passed through Auschwitz and Jerusalem.

There is little doubt or argument that all Jews should at some time or other make a journey, a pilgrimage, to Jerusalem. But since that time when the body of Israel ascended to a silent sky on columns of smoke and ash, perhaps the only way for a Jew to get to Jerusalem is by way of Auschwitz.

"I hope you understand," Mr. Slutzky said to me, "that now you have tied your fate to the fate and the memory of the Six Million."

No, Mr. Slutzky, I still do not understand. But I have made an effort to understand what cannot be understood, to understand this mystery that now makes me who I am and now announces what I must answer for. In the pages that follow, then, is some small measure of an attempt to answer.

Pilgrimage of a Proselyte

26 IYAR 5751

St. Louis, 12 May 1991

I AM SITTING IN the airport still trying to grasp the fact that I am now on my way to the Other Shore, now on my journey into silence. A remark made by Michel Foucault keeps going through my head: the madman is the Prisoner of Passage. I do not know whether I am mad, but I do know that, taking up this passage, everything around me seems somehow unreal. The place, the people, the time …Why?

The airport is crowded with men and women, young and old, speaking a variety of languages. The air is teeming with a confusion of tongues that makes my own silence all the more intense. Making my way into silence, I am passing into the heart of those tongues. Not into the silence of all tongues, mind you, but into what silences all tongues, into what strikes us dumb and sucks forth the soul in a gasp of "Can it be?" I write these lines in an effort not to fall completely mute.

"Are you ready?" my wife Gerri asked me as I left her at the Tulsa airport this morning. No, my love, I am not ready. Nor do I know how to get ready. The event, this rite of passage, is rushing along without me, and I cannot seem to catch up to it. And I am afraid. I don't want to go, but what else can I do? The invisible eyes of children grown old and the silent voices of old men as helpless as children summon me. How can I turn my back on them and remain a man?

And so I struggle to approach a place that I can never reach, to generate a presence that must necessarily miscarry. Perhaps the best I can do, what I must actually do, is engender a presence that acknowledges this terrible absence of mothers and fathers and children who should be there and yet are not. Perhaps the most I can do is become a sign not of the giving of signs but of the absence of signs.

"If their death has no meaning, then it's an outrage," one of Elie Wiesel's characters insists. "And if it does have a meaning, then it's an even greater outrage."

A sign of the absence of signs: what is the cypher-script, what is the sign, that is a sign of no sign? What is the symbol that signifies the absence of the symbol? What is the script that writes the whiteness? Even writing with invisible ink is an invasion of the void. The aircraft takes me to one place, the pen to quite another.

Can I find a way into my soul as a Jew without passing through that other Kingdom? Eyes turned to ash peer into mine and put to me the question that would return me to where I am, to who I am. Those children gaze upon me through the eyes of my own children, Miriam and Rachel, whom I have left behind so that I may return to them and impart to them a message. "Teach it to your children," we are told in the *Shma*. But what if we are unable to learn it ourselves?

"You have to write it in order to take it out," Elie told me that afternoon nearly seven years ago, when I first visited him. You have to move forward in order to come back. I am moving forward. Even as I sit here, I am moving forward and writing it down, tumbling into the page as my hand moves across it. Somehow I have to climb back out to collide with a time and a place that will put it all under erasure. And those eyes... how can so much being be crowded into such a tiny circle of darkness?

Some of the tourists around me are examining their guidebooks on Italy, so that they will know how to look upon what they shall see before they see it. I remember staring long at the ruins of Rome in the summer of 1986. "This is the way it was," they seemed to say. But the ruins of Jerusalem proclaim how it is. And what will the ruins of Treblinka, Majdanek, and Auschwitz announce? Is it possible to be a tourist in such places? The tourist goes to look. I am going to listen. I don't think that I am a tourist today. A pilgrim perhaps.

Tourist sites and tourist sights are largely aesthetic affairs. Those who gaze upon them are sensualists who would be dazzled by form, turned to stone by the face of the Medusa, which is the opposite of the face. And the pilgrim? He goes to step before the face and answer to the countenance, to hear in such a way that his hearing arises as a response. He seeks the invisible, the nameless, while the tourist cannot do without a name or a label that conforms to the categories of vision. And yet I am reminded of a Hebrew word from Rashi's* commentary on Numbers: it is *latur,* meaning "to tour," as well as "to search out." Rashi also refers to the Ark of the Covenant as the Great Searcher. Indeed, the word is a cognate of *Torah.* Perhaps in this sense the pilgrim is a tourist, one who seeks to join himself to the Great Searcher revealed in the Torah.

Prior to my departure various people commented on this trip by calling it fun, exciting, interesting.

"You're going to Poland? Oh, you must be looking for-

---

*Acronym for Rabbi Solomon ben Isaac (1040-1105), greatest of the medieval commentators on Bible and Talmud.

ward to that!"

"Israel? Oh, I bet you'll really enjoy that!"

I, of course, fled the issue and replied with my conventional nods and grins. No one said that it sounded terrifying, dangerous, overwhelming. Perhaps they were afraid to say so, just as I was afraid to depart from the script that I allowed to take the place of my voice.

I am still afraid, not of a departure from the script but of the erasure of all scripts, of the Great Absence that swallows up every word.

I am afraid of the ashes.

◊

New York, 12 May 1991

I just arrived at the TWA International Terminal at Kennedy, my third airport today. This place is one of the intersections of the world's humanity. Dostoevsky's comments on the Crystal Palace in London come to mind. You get the feeling, he said, that some event of apocalyptic proportions is imminent. An anthropologist would have to go no further to study the cultures of the world, the worlds within the world. It is a Tower of Babel to which those who were scattered have now returned. Or is it rather like the Carbide Tower of Buna that Primo Levi describes in his book *If This Is a Man,* with all the words for "brick"— *briques, teglak, mattoni, Ziegel, tegula, cegli, kamenny*—words themselves turned to bricks that erect a wall between one human being and another?

They travel in pairs, some of them, like the passengers in Noah's ark. Others move and wait and move again in families, but mostly each seems isolated from the other, and I among them, walled off from the world that juts up against the skin by the silence of my own tongue. Moving through the airport, people are careful not to touch each other. It is an unwritten rule and perhaps the nature of traveling that we remain inert in our own peculiar silence until we awaken to a face that emerges before us to open up a space that we must enter. The face speaks, and space is made of this speaking, of this address from the face of the other: Someone is asking for you. That's it, that's the feeling I cannot shake: someone is asking for me, another soul is trying to wedge its way into mine, taking me elsewhere. It is as if the more you sit still, the greater the sensation of speed.

In this small cafeteria where I am writing these notes men and women of every type sit around me, their destinations wrapped around them. Today is Mother's Day, and I am reminded that they all have mothers, someone to whom each of these souls is the most precious thing in all the world. But their mothers are far away. Here the umbilical cords are stretched to the breaking point. Do we know, can we fathom, what it means to be loved with such a love?

A child just walked past my table calling out, "Where are you? Where are you?" His question clinging to me, his frightened look terrified me. I want to answer him, but, instead, my eyes follow him until he finds the one he seeks.

We say "far away," Buber notes in *I and Thou*. But the Zulu equivalent is a sentence-word that means "there, where you cry, 'Mother, I am lost!'"

Another two hours until my flight leaves for Amsterdam. I must make a phone call. . . .

I just spoke to Elie Wiesel on the telephone. For more than ten years now I have turned to him, both to his written word and to his spoken word, when I have felt myself slipping too close to the abyss. He wished me well. "Be well," he said, his voice replete with truth and sincerity. It sounded like a blessing. "Call me when you return," he said, summoning me to answer for what I have seen before I have seen it. And he said, "Keep a diary." I told him that I have already begun a diary. Before you call, I shall answer.

So as not to be too late.

It seems that to be human is to be too late. But I am trying to catch up. In *Evil and Exile* Wiesel suggests that every
Jew take the memory of a single child, a single man or woman, who fell prey to the flames and make that memory
part of his own. "Keep a diary" is a way of saying "remember and observe," *zachor v'shamor.* Remember and make the
memory of another part of your own soul. Having adopted
the pretense of researching the memoirs of the Shoah, I
find myself being transformed into a shred of memory.

On long trips I usually take with me whatever reading
material I happen to be working through at the time. This
time it is Maimonides' *Guide for the Perplexed.* I wonder if it
can possibly guide me through the places into which I am
about to venture. One thing is certain, made clear and distinct by an unnatural light: I am thoroughly perplexed.

Why am I going? I do not know exactly. I only know
that I must. When others have asked me why I was making
such a trip, I replied, "I am going to do some research,"
and this appeared to explain everything. This is the language of the world, one that they can understand, one that
I used to think I understood.

"Ah, yes: research. Holocaust memoirs. Yes."

But as I sit here now I realize that research has nothing
to do with it. I am going in order to be undone, under-
mined, broken. How can I be a Jew and fail to go? I am
going because I was not there, because the blood of Israel
was poured out and I was not there, because God remained silent and I was not there, because all the world
remained silent and I was not there.

It happened before I was born? No excuse. It is still
happening. Darkness and silence persist in their insidious
invasion of life. I am going in order to take on a memory
not yet my own, a memory that I embraced when I became
a Jew but that I have yet to remember. I emerged from the
mikvah precisely in order to make this pilgrimage, to

breathe in the ashes, to stoop and search the ash for an ember of my brother and thus to ignite with the fire of his memory.

But who can understand such explanations? Who can understand any explanation? No, it does not belong to the understanding. I do not understand it myself. Maimonides, like Bachya* and Saadia Gaon** before him, cites three sources of knowledge: reason, Torah, and tradition. But it transcends even that.

An elderly Orthodox Jew is standing at the gate where the flight for London is now boarding. His beard is long and gray from years of poring over Torah and Talmud, and his dress is a signifier of his relation to the One who rules every relation that goes into his life. Under his arm he carries a small bag containing, no doubt, the *siddur* (prayerbook), the *talit,* and the *tefillin* that he will take out for his morning *shacharit* prayers during the flight across the Atlantic. It is quite warm in the airport, and so he has removed his black hat to reveal a black *kipah,* a sign of his devotion to the Holy One, blessed be He.

My *kipah* is tucked safely in my shirt pocket.

---

*Bachya ben Joseph ibn Pakuda, twelfth-century thinker, author of *Duties of the Heart.*

**Saadia ben Joseph ha-Fayyum (852-942), last of the great heads of the Babylonian Talmudic academies and author of *The Book of Beliefs and Opinions.*

29 IYAR 5751

Amsterdam, 13 May 1991

ALREADY **I** AM LEARNING what it means to be a Jew by learning what it means to be a man. And it was a man who is surely not a Jew that taught me this. On the flight from New York to Amsterdam there was a young couple—in their late twenties, I would say—with two children, a little girl no more than two years of age and an infant perhaps only a month old. They had purchased two seats for the four of them. In one narrow, economy-class seat the mother sat cradling the babe curled up in the comfort of her love. In the other, a seat on the aisle, the two-year-old slept while her father stood watch over her, stood without a break throughout the night crossing, never taking a rest, never leaving his feet. Like a man standing seven hours for the *Amidah,* the silent prayer whose name means "standing."

As I looked upon this amazing yet unimposing man, it struck me that his standing was itself a kind of prayer. As he stood, he stood for something, a sign of the profound significance of the tiny other who lay in the seat before him. Thus signifying the depth and the dearness of the little one, he himself took on a depth that I fear I may never achieve. He stood without a trace of any resentment that might have marked his fatherly face. The only thing to be seen in those eyes was a profound caring coupled with a sense of protection: nothing that lurked in the night would come near his little girl.

That young father, who clearly knows far more than I might hope to understand, reminded me of one important point to my pilgrimage. If I learn nothing more than how to stand watch over my children through the night, then I shall have learned more than I could ever expect to learn. I thought of the nights when my baby girls would call out to me, and I would go to them, take them in my arms, and repeat over and over to them, "It's all right. Papa is right here. It's all right." Then I would walk them back to sleep. But I never stood over them for a seven-hour vigil. I wondered whether I was capable of what seemed to come without effort to that young father. Yes, already I am learning a great deal.

I spent the night reading the *Moreh Nevuchim,* Rambam's* *Guide,* looking up now and then to the father who unknowingly guided me through a great deal. Seeing him with his family made me ache for my daughters, for my wife. Already I miss them terribly. Already I am overwhelmed with something that I had not expected: gratitude. I recall the Hasidic Rebbe whose greatest fear was that he might not be able to show God his gratitude, and I understand him a little better. And I recall Moshe Leib's** injunction to himself: "Don't just tell God of your fear and your hunger. Tell Him how *grateful* you are."

Judah Halevi says in *The Kuzari* that three things draw us nigh unto the Holy One: love, fear, and joy. And, I think, the key to all three is gratitude. It is gratitude that

---

*Acronym for Rabbi Moshe ben Maimon, or Maimonides.
**Moshe Leib of Sassov (1744-1807), Hasidic rabbi.

enables us to behold the invisible treasure lying at our feet, hugging us around the neck, or curled up asleep on a flight over the ocean.

It is true: we are addressed in all things. In silent things most deeply. For those who have ears to hear, deep unceasingly calls unto deep.

Rosh Hodesh Sivan

Warsaw, 14 May 1991

IT IS 3:20 IN THE morning. Naturally, I cannot sleep.

I arrived in Warsaw yesterday evening at around five o'clock. Going through Customs was easy. All they wanted to know was how much money I had. Outside the terminal dozens of men out of work were trying to hustle some dollars by offering their own private taxi service. One man came up to me and told me that for ten dollars he would take me anywhere in the city. I told him I was going to the Novotel Hotel. He nodded, took my bag, and we were on our way.

"Politic in Poland very good," he told me. "No more communist. But economic very bad."

Fifteen minutes later I was in the hotel. Exhausted, I went down at 7:30.

Everything here is gray, the sky overhead a cloudless gray, the buildings, the people, all gray, all the color of despair. Or is it just me?

But these are details that have nothing to do with what drove me to my notebook. In the course of my sleep I suddenly awoke crying uncontrollably. It was unlike anything

I have ever experienced before. The spasms of tears have subsided, but throughout my body I still feel the aftereffects. Yes, like everyone, I have had bad dreams—dreams of some harm coming to my little girls, Miriam and Rachel. But then I would quickly realize that it was just that, a bad dream, thank God, they were safe in their beds, thank God. And I would go back to sleep. Like everyone else.

Not this time. The dream was not about my children, exactly. I am not even sure that it was a dream. A vision, perhaps, of the sort that terrified Job: "Thou afrightest me with dreams and visions." No, it was not about my children, at least not in any direct way, but it had something to do with children. I cannot recall it in much detail. I don't know whether that is good or bad. I do remember heaps of stones—or was it a field of stones?—and in the midst of them a deep pit. Where the children were or what they had to do with the stones and the pit, I cannot say. Or maybe I am afraid to say.

The next thing I recall is that I was suddenly weeping, first in the dream and then when I awoke. And for several minutes I could not stop, as though the tears were not coming from me but I was being drawn along on the current of the tears. I don't remember any particular incident in the dream. I was just weeping over the children, over this place where the sky itself weeps, weeps tears of blood, like in Piotr Rawicz's novel *Blood From the Sky*. The tear-shaped stone comes to mind, the one I picked up at Dachau five years ago and have carried with me ever since. God's tear.

Once I began to recover, the words my father spoke just before I left came back to me: Don't panic. I managed to calm myself by repeating those words that my father offered to me. Even now he was coming to my aid, as he always has. At the time—was it only two days ago?—when he said to me, "Don't panic," I was a bit puzzled. After all, this was my sixth crossing of the Atlantic on my own, and prior to none of those other trips did he ever make such a remark to me. Now I understand why he offered me those words, that lifeline, even though he perhaps did not know what he was saying or why he said it.

There is a great tension within me, in the air around me, in the ground beneath me, like the tension in a thread that is about to break but is not yet broken. Part of it, I think, is a tension between attending to the business of getting to the places I have come to encounter and... nearing the edge of tears, horror, collapse. And part of it is perhaps a tension between what I am and what I am about to become. It is like taking too big a dose of a bad drug and trying to get yourself through it by saying to yourself, "It's only the drug. It'll pass. Don't panic." But it isn't the drug. There is no drug. Or rather the "drug" is what you clamber to get back into, the illusory reality of "all is well" that we fashion in our flight from a truth that stirs panic and terror. Can this be the God who *is*, the Tetragrammaton* that Rambam describes in terms of fear and trembling?

Today is the first of Sivan. It is the 45th day in the Counting of the Omer. On this day begins the month in which the Torah was given at Mount Sinai. There is the silence that preceded the Creation, Elie Wiesel has said, and the silence of Mount Sinai. The first signifies chaos and solitude, the second presence and plenitude. Which one is this silence that now steals over me?

I wrapped my *talit* around me and put on my *tefillin* this morning. The sun was up before five o'clock. My prayers have given me strength and light. "Hear, O Israel.... Blessed is He who alone brings us peace...." Thus He heals our wounds and makes us whole, *shalem* by His *shalom*. This is the Holy One of whom Rambam speaks, the

---

*The four letters of the Holy Name: *yud hay vav hay*.

one whose essence is existence, whose name is the Tetra-grammaton. And yet...

I am setting out now for Treblinka.

◊

On the Train to Treblinka

Although my stay in Poland has been brief, so far I have met mostly with kindness from the people around me. In the Central Train Station, for example, I was trying to get information about trains going to and from Treblinka. The woman in the Information Booth, of course, spoke no English. Almost no one outside of the hotel, it seems, speaks English, and already the silence of being stranded outside of the native tongue is oppressive. When I try speaking Russian, I usually meet with cold intolerance, perhaps due to memories of an intolerant regime; yes, it is amazing, even frightening, what a word can convey.

But the Russian tongue is the only means of communication that I have at my disposal. So I was conversing with the woman in Russian, a language that seemed to leave a bad taste on her tongue, when, seeing my difficulty, a young man who spoke some English came to my aid. With his assistance, I finally determined that in order to get to Treblinka I had to leave from the Gdansk Station. So here I am, thanks to his help, on the train to Treblinka. I did not even get his name.

Riding this train, I cannot help recalling other trains, those that departed from the *Umschlagplatz* (the site from which trains departed for the death camp) in the Warsaw Ghetto, as well as from elsewhere. Unlike the men, women, and children who rode those trains, I am carrying a round-trip ticket. We have just crossed the Vistula. Looking now upon these woods, these rails, a memory other than my own creeps over me. I think of the eyes for whom these sights were the last, those that took their last look at the city, the river, the towns along the way, their vision dimmed by terror.

The train just passed by a building with a huge swastika painted on its roof. I caught the words *ueber alles*. Is it possible? Was it really there? Or was it some terrible phantom from those days when the Angel of Death swept through this land? The tragedy, Wiesel once wrote, is not that the possible proves to be impossible but that the impossible turns out to be possible.

We are rolling past old train cars parked along the tracks, the ones with the small windows in the upper corners that used to be covered with barbed wire. Who has not seen the photographs of those who were condemned to death for being alive peering out of these windows? A shudder runs through me at the sight of them. They are every bit old enough to have been among the train cars used to carry God's Chosen to their deaths some fifty years ago. And if they are old enough to have been used, you may be sure that they were used. How many unanswered cries rose up and died away within the confines of those cars? How many, indeed, died in those very cars that now sit so silently along the track to Treblinka?

I change trains in Malkenia, just five kilometers from the stop marked "Treblinka." Who has not seen the photographs?

§

Treblinka

I sit here, another stone in a meadow covered with stones rooted to this ash-covered earth. I sit alone. There is no one else here, except for a couple of peasant women pulling the weeds from between some of the stones in the distance. I listen for the voices I came to hear, but I hear no voices. Just a muted, mechanical rumbling of indifference, neither being nor nothingness, a noise that persists after the cessation of every other noise. It cuts through the air like these jagged stones that make up a forest of stones in the midst of this Polish forest overflowing with the rumbling silence. Slowly, silently, the tears come to my eyes, roll down my cheeks and into my beard. They rise with the rising of the stones, and just as ineluctably.

When I got off at the Treblinka train stop, there was no one and nothing around. I had expected at least some indication of the way to the camp, but…nothing. I approached an old house about a hundred feet off the tracks. A dog came out barking at me, followed by an old woman and her husband. Before I said a word, they knew exactly what I had come for.

"Lager?" the woman asked.

"Yes, please," I answered in the few Polish words I knew and then asked in my apologetic Russian how to get there.

She made some gestures toward a country road that ran alongside the tracks and in Polish repeated, "Five kilometers, five kilometers." Seeing my look of uncertainty, her husband drew a map in the dirt. Noting that they had to be past sixty years of age, I wondered where they had been when the world was turned on end. I politely thanked them and set out down the road.

Horse-drawn carts hauling everything from carrots to coal passed me along the way to my destination. Nearing a village that lies next to the site of the death camp, I stopped to look at an aged roadside shrine to the Virgin Mary. Had this image graven in stone been here when people were going up in flames just a stone's throw away? She would not answer.

I pressed on, making my way through the village called Poniatowo, a name that means "understood." In a place called Understood, it struck me, "good" people, baptized Christians all, stood by and did nothing as the trains lum-

bered, one after another, through their town. Our Town.
Every Town. Quaint, curious, and contaminated by the
smoke and ash that settled on their roofs and in their nos-
trils. They were close enough to have heard the screams in
the night, to have awakened from bad dreams and gone
back to sleep. It was here, in fact, that the infamous Ivan
the Terrible, perhaps the man called Demjanjuk, came on
his days off to sleep with a villager's wife. Then he would
rise from her bed and her body to return to his task of
herding Jewish bodies into the gas chamber.

Just the other side of Poniatowo I came to the entrance
to the site of the death camp. Along the road, between the
road and the railroad tracks, now covered with dark green
shrubs, there was a mass grave perhaps two hundred feet
long and about thirty feet wide. And its depth, no doubt,
goes to the center of the earth. Next to it stood four or
five men, sentries who ignored me as I crossed over the
tracks and went up a smaller road that turned off the
country road.

After walking about half a kilometer through the forest, I finally arrived at the clearing arrayed with the
jagged stones, where now I sit. I was relieved to find that,
although there is a small building that sells a few booklets
from a window, there are no guides, no guide books, no
box office selling tickets to the attraction—in short, nothing to insulate or protect you from the wounds that this
place inflicts upon the soul. In fact, the window was
closed when I arrived here.

Not a fragment, not a stick, of the camp's wooden
structures remains. After the uprising that took place in
the camp on August 2, 1943, the Nazis destroyed everything that had stood here. All that is left is the silence of
these stones and the ash covering the soil from which they
jut into the air like petrified screams. Each one is posi-
tioned as a *matzeva*, each a grave marker where there are
no graves, where the grounds are themselves one huge

grave.

Many of the stones bear the names of families and whole communities that perished in this place. On some are written the names of individuals, like Janusz Korczak, the doctor who ran a Jewish orphanage in Warsaw and who chose to go to his death with the children when he could have saved himself; he had the courage and the wisdom to realize that saving himself when his children were being sent to their deaths would have meant losing himself and his soul.

Just off the center of this field of stones there is what appears to be the remains of a pit used to burn the bodies of the dead. It is covered with black stones that resemble charred pieces of timber, and in the depths of that pit... the children. Suddenly I am face to face with the dream that sent me into convulsions of tears early this morning. Don't panic, David.

I have been here for nearly two hours now, walking the grounds, caressing the stones, and muttering through my tears the prayers for the dead. I don't think I can take much more of it. Besides, a small van filled with Polish teenagers has just pulled into the camp.

They are so talkative. Why? What is there to say in this place, except perhaps a *Kaddish* and a cry of "God, forgive me!" No more, please!

◊

On the Train Back to Warsaw

I started to walk back to the Treblinka train stop and had just left the entrance to the camp, when two men, Polish peasants, stopped and offered me a ride. The driver was between thirty-five and forty years of age, dressed in old clothes and in need of a shave. The man sitting next to him was around sixty. He wore very thick glasses and had only one nostril; in the place of the other nostril there was a V-shaped hole that ran halfway up his nose. For some reason—perhaps because I was a bit weary from all the walking I had done—I accepted the offer and got in the backseat.

No sooner did they start up the car than I realized that both of them were drunk. They raced through Poniatowo, swerving around pedestrians and horse-drawn carts, and soon reached the Treblinka train stop. There the driver stopped at the side of the road, turned off the engine, and got out to urinate. He told me to stay in the car and said that he would take me to Malkenia. By that time, however, I was afraid to go any further with them, given their inebriated condition, and I too got out of the car, with the older man right behind me. I was afraid for other reasons as well.

"Yisraeli?" the driver had asked me along the way.

Thinking he was asking me if I was an Israeli, I answered, "No, American."

"Nay, nay, Yisraeli, Yisraeli," he repeated, pointing to the *kipah* in my shirt pocket. I had worn it while walking the grounds of the death camp Treblinka. Then he gestured toward my beard (Poles generally do not wear beards) and said, "You Yisraeli, we Polski."

Realizing that they had recognized me as a Jew, I did not deny anything. It would have been pointless. But I did wonder what they thought of my being a Jew. Stories of Jews who escaped from Treblinka and Sobibor only to be killed by Polish peasants flashed through my mind. No, I did not deny anything. It was too late, thank God, for denial to be an option. But then, as terrible as it is to confess, I did not affirm, "Yes, I am a Jew." I had come to Poland, today to Treblinka, to affirm my Jewishness, and at the first sign of danger I failed to declare, "Yes, I am a Jew!"

As I stood with them at the side of the road, they kept

urging me to get back into the car with them, assuring me that they were good people. The driver asked me if I was carrying any money, any dollars, and the man with one nostril wanted to know if I had a camera in my bag. All the while they were calling me "Yisraeli," as if it were my name, a name I could not refuse, a name that called me out into the open and demanded a response.

After a few minutes of politely refusing their offer to show me that they were good people, I started walking toward the train tracks next to the sign that read "Treblinka." I turned my back to them and headed for the train stop, and still they shouted after me, "Yisraeli, Yisraeli!" For a few steps I tried to ignore them. Then, recalling that God would not allow even the bones of Moses to be carried into the Promised Land because he had denied being a Hebrew when he fled to Midian, I hesitatingly turned in response to the name and waved them off.

Still, I had not said, "Yes, I am a Jew," and a part of me was afraid for having been recognized as a Jew. A part of me was more afraid of these two drunken Poles than of God. How can I ever atone for this sin or get past this shame? Only minutes after walking through the stones of the death camp I betrayed the children who were murdered there. God, God, please forgive me! But how can You?

I breathed a sigh of relief and disgrace when they got back into their car and drove off toward Malkenia.

After waiting for a short while at the train stop, I went up to the house where the old couple lived to ask when the next train was due to stop here. Again the kind woman who spoke no English and only a little Russian came out and explained to me that no train stops here on the way back to Malkenia. She told me that I would have to walk the five kilometers to Malkenia. And so I set out once more down the country road. Along the way I was overwhelmed at the thought that I had been sold a round-trip ticket to Treblinka, a place for which there is no round trip.

On the road to Malkenia peasants riding in carts laden with coal eyed me suspiciously and did not respond to my greetings. Did they too spot me as a Jew? Between Treblinka and Malkenia there is a fairly wide river spanned by a very narrow bridge. As I walked across it, I had the sensation that it might collapse at any moment. Judgment, we are told in the Talmud, occurs on a bridge. And I knew what judgment I had merited. Once again, fear sliced through my soul like a razor, but this time it was fear of God.

God in His infinite mercy, however, continued to smile on me, despite my cowardice in the face of the two drunkards, for just as I arrived at the Malkenia station, the train for Warsaw pulled up. At least I think it is the train for Warsaw. I climbed aboard and am sitting in it now.

I cannot get over this guilt over having failed to announce to the drunken Polish peasants that, yes, I am a Jew. Another terrible truth: as I was entering the site of the death camp, I hesitated for a moment before putting on my *kipah*, for fear that I might be seen to be a Jew. But I put it on anyway. In that place it was impossible not to wear it. Other hands guided my hands as I put it firmly on my head.

But as soon as I left the grounds I put it back into my shirt pocket. Yes, it could be seen—the two drunkards saw it—but it is not so obvious as when it is on my head. Which am I to do? Hide from men the fact that I am a Jew, or show to God my devotion to Him as a Jew? Keeping the *kipah* in my shirt pocket is a feeble way of trying to have it both ways. It is a coward's way, a half measure that proves to be empty, a half truth that proves to be false. When and where will I find the courage to do it God's way?

Again the stories run through my mind: Jews rose up in the death camps at Sobibor and Treblinka and escaped the

Nazi murderers only to be murdered by the peasants in villages like Poniatowo and Malkenia. I put on the *kipah* while treading the ashes that cover the site of the death camp and melodramatically thought to myself that if I might ever be ridiculed or even injured for being a Jew, then this was the place for it—if, indeed, there can be a place for it. I know that it is wrong to invite persecution for being a Jew; the Jews need anything but more victims. But I also know that it is wrong to flee from danger when the flight from it means a flight from being a Jew.

When the reality became too real and the drunk turned to me and said "Yisraeli?" I took flight, shook my head, and answered, "No, American." The question that haunts me now is this: When I said, "No, American," did I mean to say, "No, I'm not a Jew"? I did not say that, but still… was I trying to pass for something else? If so, then, in trying to pass for something else, did I become something else?

Like Rebbe Zusya,* I shall stand one day before the Celestial Tribunal, another Bet Din, and they will ask me not "Why weren't you Jacob?" or "Why weren't you Moses?" but "Why weren't you Avraham David, if that is who you are? Are you indeed Avraham David? Avraham David *ben Avraham* ?" And I am terrified of the answer. There is no place of grace for those who turn away from the face, no time to rejoice for those who hear and deny the Voice.

I am acquiring a disquieting education in the problem of presence: in this place, much of the time, I do not know where I shall be or what will transpire an hour from the moment at hand. It is true that all of us are continually confronted with such a situation, but we usually have enough illusions at our disposal to dispel the reality of this not-knowing-beforehand. Here in Poland, however, I find

---

*Meshullam Zusya of Annopol (d. 1800), Hasidic master.

myself in a situation that will not accommodate much in the way of illusions. My distance from the language, among other things, removes me from such handrails. The language itself erects the signposts that tell us where to go and what to anticipate; when the language is lost, we lose the markers that point the way for us. Here the language is not lost, but I am lost to the language.

I am reminded of the sign along the road from the Treblinka train stop to the site of the concentration camp, the sign posted as a warning of a curve up ahead: anyone driving that stretch of road, going in that direction, would come to the sign only *after* having negotiated the curve. It is a truly existential sign: the warnings always come after the event. That is what Poland is for the outsider—an existential country whose signs are readable only when it is too late, a country phenomenologically out of step, staggering like the drunks that you see here at every turn, and only after you have negotiated the turn.

◊

Warsaw

I am back in my room, exhausted and ashamed. How can I move beyond this guilt over the incident with the two peasants? Or is it better not to move beyond it?

A short while ago I had a brief chat with another drunkard in the hotel lobby. We spoke a mixture of Russian, German, and French, twisting the languages into mangled sentences in the midst of this twisted realm. He too wanted me to go with him, to his apartment, where we could have a good talk. Did he spot me as a Jew? Perhaps. He pointed out some men who were standing not far from us and claimed that they were Iraqis. He said that he wanted to kill them, that he wanted to kill all Arabs. Then he looked into my eyes for an approval that I refused to give him. At least I am still enough of a Jew not to join in a cry of "Death to the Arabs!"

2 *Sivan* 5751

Warsaw, 15 May 1991

THIS APPEARS TO BE the place for nightmares, for last night I had another one. This time it was about a huge mechanical monster, mechanical but alive. It was chasing me, trying to take me into its gullet. As I ran from it across a stretch of dirt, I could see a barbed-wire fence in the distance. I ran faster, hoping I could reach the fence and somehow climb over it before the thing could catch me. I made it to the fence and started climbing, struggling to work my way through a space between the strands of barbed wire, but I could not manage it. Suddenly I realized that someone else—a woman, I think—was climbing with me, also unable to squeeze through the wire. I tried to help her, knowing that with every second the monster was closing in on us. Then, when it had nearly reached us, the metallic creature abruptly came to a halt.

"He has changed his mind," the woman explained to me. "Maybe he has had enough."

In the Mishnah it is written that a dream uninterpreted is like a letter unopened. But I am not sure what the message might be in this one. Perhaps it is about the extreme

57

anxiety I feel in this land where so many Jews have been swallowed up by a monstrous, inhuman machine known as anti-Semitism. And I am not convinced that the anti-Semitism is gone. Perhaps the woman was my soul telling me not to be afraid. Or maybe the monster is the guilt over my cowardice that will not let go of me. Maybe it is a dream that I have inherited, like a memory, from the dead.

When I took out my *tefillin* this morning I discovered a very thoughtful card that my wife had slipped into my luggage. She put it with my *tefillin*, knowing that there I would be sure to find it. I don't know why or how I could have missed it yesterday when I prepared to recite the morning prayers. Perhaps the message of her love was intended to wait until I had a greater need for it. Like the *tefillin*, her note was a word, a sign, binding me to what is most dear, most blessed. This is the sign that I lay on my arm to guide my hand, that I place between my eyes to help me to see.

She told me not to worry about our little girls, like the voice of my soul that appeared in my dream. When I am away from home I always have a much greater sense of what it means to trust in God to watch over my little ones. It isn't easy. I often feel helpless even when I am there to look after them. But when I am so far away...

Today I shall attempt to go to Lublin, the home of the Holy Seer,* and from there proceed to Majdanek. As I prepare to set out, a story about the Seer comes to mind, the tale of his Great Fall, as it is called. It seems that one night, after ordering the members of his congregation to dance and sing with a fervor such as they had never shown before, he retired to his study on the second floor of the synagogue. Suddenly a disciple who stood vigil by his closed door heard a terrible scream coming from inside

---

*Rabbi Jacob Hurwitz (1745-1815), Hasidic master.

the Rabbi's room. Fearing for the Master's life, the young man rushed in to find that the Seer had disappeared. A number of his followers went outside to look for him in the streets of Lublin. Finally, in an alley not far from the synagogue, they found him lying on the ground.

"Master, what happened?" they wanted to know. "Are you all right? What did you see? Was it the Evil One?" What, indeed, could have spirited the Seer from the room?

But all the old man could answer was, "The abyss calls for another abyss...the abyss..."

It is time for me to go. The abyss calls my name.

◈

On the Train to Lublin

I think I am sitting on the train for Lublin. We have just pulled out of the Gdansk Station.

Traveling like this entails a lot of waiting. One must learn to sit still. The difficulty surrounding that lies in dealing with all the thoughts, apprehensions, and imaginations that invade your soul. They come whether you like it or not, against your will. Sitting still requires not only patience but the kind of faith that we pray for each day, the peace, the *shalom*, that can come only from God, as it is said in the closing lines of the *Amidah*.

"Don't worry," my wife assured me. "Everything will be fine at home. I love you."

And the words of my father return to me: "Don't panic."

As I sit still and gaze upon the beauty of the Polish countryside, my loved ones sit with me. And so my heart is stilled.

◈

Lublin, 15 May 1991

It is noon, and I have arrived at the Uno Hotel. It is situated adjacent to the Catholic University, the one private institution of higher education in Poland. The next task: to get to Majdanek. Yesterday Treblinka. Today Majdanek. It is too much, far too much. But the same old question keeps hitting me in the face: what else can I do?

There was no way to get to Treblinka, except by walking the five kilometers from the train stop, or perhaps by hiring a private car. We'll see what it takes to get to Majdanek. Whatever it takes.

§

Majdanek

The site of the death camp Majdanek lies near the last stop on the bus line that runs through Lublin. The desk clerk at the hotel was kind enough to give me a ticket to get here and back.

Now that I am here, I don't know what to say or where to begin. This place is beyond all horizons, one of the ends of the earth that swallows up every word that might try to capture it. To speak of it would only increase the distance that isolates it from humanity and humanity from itself. But, as afraid as I am of this speaking, I am even more afraid of remaining silent.

There are only four or five people on the grounds. Like Treblinka, it is not a tourist attraction. Those who perished here have been spared at least that much. As soon as I came onto the site, I stood transfixed before the huge stone monolith that stands at the main entrance. It is made of shapes, or the remnants of shapes, that resemble the broken letters of an unidentifiable alphabet. The letters try to form a word, but the word will not come. Perhaps it is the name of God. Here that word—and with it every word—has died, died by murder, its ashes sent up the chimney of the crematorium that looms in the distance, up the chimney and into the air by which we breathe, by which we speak.

All is silent. Through the rectangular passageway cut into the monolith I see a road about two kilometers long. It runs along what used to be the electrified fence that borders the camp. Every couple of hundred feet there are wooden watchtowers overlooking the rows of silent barracks that still stand. On the opposite side of the road there is a farm, its fields dotted with crows that soar over the camp like lost souls. Here and there they alight on the barbed wires of the once-deadly fence. Atop a hill at the end of the road there is a large concrete dome, a mausoleum, and next to the mausoleum stands the crematorium. Three high school girls, from Lublin it seems, are walking the road ahead of me. They too are silent.

As I near the mausoleum, it looms even larger than I had thought it to be. A sign at the steps leading up to this structure that resembles something from another world says that here, in the open air under this massive concrete dome, are piled the ashes of the dead of Majdanek. Somehow I manage to find the strength to ascend the steps and approach the mound of ashes that sleep their troubled sleep beneath the dome.

Scattered over the mound I can see fragments of bone, traces of human being etched into this nothingness. Leaning against the short concrete wall that separates me from the ashes, I am overwhelmed by a terrible temptation to dive into the ashes, to cover myself with them, to place a handful in my mouth and thus find a way to let them speak. And an image rises up before my eyes: it is the man who threw himself on top of a mass grave that covered his family, his entire community, and begged the dead not to refuse him.

I think the only thing that stopped me from imitating that man was the fact that the sides of the structure that housed the ashes were slanted and polished as smooth as a mirror. Once inside of that mirror, it would be impossible to climb out. Yes, impossible: once you entered those ashes, there could be no returning from them. Suddenly it struck me that I was gazing into the abyss that gazed into the Holy Seer, the abyss that calls for another abyss. You don't look upon the ashes—they look upon you, look into you and cut into you to open up a wound for which there is no healing. Bending over the edge of the wall that separated me from the ashes, I took a deep breath, and drew into my lungs a trace of that life turned to dust, making myself into its urn.

After reciting the *Kaddish,* I slowly turned to face the crematorium, that factory whose product had been these ashes. Heading toward it with a slow and reverent gait, I had the sensation that at any moment now the ground would crumble out from under my feet. Perhaps, indeed, it already has. It has crumbled into the mountain of ash that is covered by a concrete dome dozens of feet across, crumbled into that broken reflection of the Twentieth Century.

The first room you come to inside of the crematorium is the dissection room, where gold was removed from the speechless mouths of the dead, as if those stiffened, gaping jaws opened up caverns to be mined for their wealth. A bouquet of withered flowers lies on top of the table where the miners did their heinous work. Is it possible that the hands that mined those mouths and the hands that placed those flowers here both belonged to human beings, to the same creature created in the image of God? Is this the impossible that turns out to be possible?

After lingering over those withered flowers, I walked on until I came to the gas chamber. I peered inside of it without going in, peered and listened for the echoes of screams that rebounded off these walls and settled over the dead. If walls have ears, then how, in God's Holy Name, can these walls still be standing? I did not go in because I was afraid of what I might hear, afraid that I might never come out.

I walked a few steps further and came to a room that housed cadavers waiting to be fed into the ovens. In the center of the room is a heap of bones under a glass display case. They tell more about this place, about this unbearably immense space, than all the signs in four different languages posted about the walls. These bones belie the impotence of all languages to tell it. Son of Man, can these bones rise and live again? Will they roll their way to Jerusalem on the Last Day and there be reassembled? And if so, what can the Holy One, blessed be He, possibly have to say to them?

A step or two and a turn to the left: the ovens. There are five of them. I see that they are filled with ashes, and my eyes fill with tears. For some reason Isaac comes to mind: he went blind, the Midrash tells us, because the tears of an angel fell into his eyes as he lay upon the altar at Mount Moriah. What angels have shed their tears in this very room? Here even the Angel of Death, the Angel with a Thousand Eyes, would weep at the sight. I look, but I cannot focus. My head is reeling. I stretch out my hands to restore my balance, to reach for something that isn't there. I cannot say how long I stood there groping like a blind man. But it was only long enough for my legs to come back to me and carry me away from the blinding sight, away from the deafening silence.

When I finally left the crematorium, I walked back down the road and around the perimeter to the other side of the camp, where a dozen or so barracks house exhibits.

Along the way I passed a boy of about ten walking up the hill toward the mausoleum. He had a skateboard under his arm.

Arriving at the entrance to this portion of the camp, I

was thankful once again that there were no tours, no guides or guide books. Just the stark, terrifying, unsheathed reality of the place. The first block I came to housed another gas chamber. And next to the gas chamber is a second chamber, a very small chamber with a peephole looking into the gas chamber. There SS men, men who had wives and children of their own, stood and looked on as the wives and children of other men breathed their gasping, choking last. They looked and gawked and stared, unable to avert their gaze, entranced by the scene that surpassed anything dreamt of in Dante's *Inferno*.

How is it that these men were not turned into pillars of salt? How, by what right, and in the name of what did they not go insane? Or had they already gone mad, as the world had gone mad? Following their orders, they took notes and kept records and then went home to bounce their little ones on their knees and make love to their wives. I do not understand these words that I write.

Coming out of the block, I understand even less. For just over there, just the other side of the fence, there is a group of children playing. They live in the apartment buildings that come right up to the edge of the camp. *How* do they live in those buildings next to these buildings? What do their mothers and fathers say to them when they ask, as children do, "What is that, Mommy?"

I move on to the line of barracks housing exhibits. Across from them is a statue of a woman raising her infant up to the heavens. Or is she snatching her babe from the heavens, from the silence of a sky occluded by smoke and ash? Gazing upon this image of mother and child, I head for the barracks and the exhibits they hold, now this one, now the next, in no particular order.

I go into one and find that it is filled with shoes piled several feet deep, shoes of every description, work shoes for men who would never show up for work, dress shoes for women whose evenings had turned into one long night, shoes like those I had seen my grandparents wear, shoes worn...on tiny feet that never had a chance to outgrow them.

I go into a second block, and it too is piled waist-deep with shoes that used to tread the streets of Europe.

I go into a third: more shoes. How many can there be? I cannot fathom the number, and it seems as though they are walking over me, walking through me, filling my soul with the ghosts of the humanity whose feet they covered. Old wounds in my legs begin to ache, and I feel that I have been struck lame, like Jacob when he wrestled with the angel at Peniel. Who would have thought that shoes could tell so much?

I stagger into another block and find it filled with clothing on one side and the striped prisoners' uniforms on another, the clothes that unmade the man and covered him with the bars of his imprisonment. No matter where he went, he moved within the confines of his cell. Still another block is lined on the right side with the striped prisoners' caps and on the left with the hats stolen from the deportees before they were slowly murdered.

I say "stolen" and "murdered," yet the language of criminality strikes me as empty, trite understatement. Here every overstatement of the horror is an understatement. Here you not only behold the evidence of the crime—you can *smell* it oozing out of the open doors of the barracks that now house the raiment that once covered only a few of those who went up the chimney. The odor from this clothing crawls into your own clothing and follows you, like a shadow, from their grave all the way to your own. Once again I hear the echo of the abyss that calls unto another abyss. It is the sound of Jew calling unto Jew.

That is what Majdanek is: a place made of one abyss upon another. An abyss of Jewish shoes that covered Jewish feet whose footsteps ended here, feet that trod a ground that swallowed them up. Along the wall of yet another block there are dozens of empty canisters embossed with a death's head and the word *Zyklon-B*, signifying the gas pellets that had robbed the shoes of the feet they were meant to cover, feet that would have no more need of those shoes.

And behind the blocks children play, children wearing shoes and clothing and caps that, God willing, they would soon outgrow. In the distance, where the crows are flying overhead, looms the smokestack that consumed a thousand or more each day, day after day, death after death. It cuts a wound into the sky over the hill, where it stands next to the concrete dome that covers the ashes swept from the bowels of the chimney, O the chimney, and Israel's children riding the wind to spread their remains over the face of earth and sea!

Again the sky is overcast, eternally overcast, like a spell cast over this land, as if the clouds of smoke continued to blot out the sun and devour the light. Standing here, devastated, on this site where tens and hundreds of thousands of Jews were consumed, I am reminded of my mission: I came to this place as a Jew, or as one struggling to become a Jew. I came to be undone, to undergo a circumcision of the soul. Standing on this soil made of Jewish remains, I feel the shame over my cowardice in the face of the drunken peasants once more take hold of my throat.

But it seems that my encounter with the fear of being marked as a Jew was a necessary part of my collision with what took place on this sacred ground, this terrible ground soaked with Jewish blood that silently shrieks unto a sky transformed into a cemetery. I had to know, I was blessed by *HaShem* with knowing, if only for a moment, what it meant to be spotted as a Jew in the Polish countryside, to feel threatened, to be called "Yisraeli" and thus to be marked as *other*. In a way, perhaps, a man cannot be a Jew in this world without having been frightened or having felt threatened at being recognized as a Jew. And it happened to me, by the grace of God, just a couple of hundred feet from the train stop marked *Treblinka.*

Do I now know anything more of what was known to those fathers and mothers and children who wore the shoes piled up in the barracks of Majdanek? Certainly not. God protect me from such presumption. But perhaps when I was afraid of being labeled a Jew I caught a faint taste of a single instant of what for them had been an eternal torment. In my daily prayers, like all Jews who pray, I ask for *chochmah, binah,* and *daat*—wisdom, understanding, and knowledge. Although my ignorance remains, I have perhaps been blessed with an atom of what I pray for. And perhaps I have been rightly punished for my presumption.

Tonight begins the 47th day in the counting of the Omer. I shall count and anticipate the Sixth of Sivan, which I shall spend in this land so far away from Sinai, if it is God's will. But then I look around at this place and ask, "What, indeed, is the will of God?"

3 Sivan 5751

Lublin, 16 May 1991

MOSHE BEN MAIMON, in his *Guide for the Perplexed,* speaks of a precious treasure that underlies all life. It occurs to me that Majdanek has been transformed into the memorial it is now by virtue of that treasure. For Majdanek is no longer a death camp but the *site* of a death camp, a place where we go to have our memories jarred and our souls undone for the sake of the precious treasure that underlies life. It is a place marked for the remembrance and observance of what is most dear in life. It is a place, therefore, that has been remade into an affirmation of life *because* and *in spite of* the death that reigned there.

No longer are hats exchanged for striped caps. Now you enter and cover your head with a *kipah* as you gaze upon those hats that fill an entire block. Now you walk carefully among those piles of shoes, knowing that the shoes you wear have been consecrated by their contact with that terrible, hallowed ground. Now you realize that all ground is hallowed by the treasure that underlies it and by the ashes that cover it. This, of course, cannot justify even a single death, a single tear shed, in the death camp

Majdanek. It is beyond justification and explanation. Why? Because a precious treasure underlies life. All life.

Still, I cannot shake the feeling that a Jew has no place here in Poland. And I begin to realize a bit more about the significance of Erets Yisrael and why it is at the center of the circles of holiness that sanctify all life in the world. Israel is not just another nation in a world of nations. Why, indeed, does such a small land with such a small population command so much of the world's attention? It is because Israel signifies and makes possible human dwelling in any land. In Poland some three and a half million Jews once made God—the One known as *HaMakom,* or the Place—their dwelling place. There were some, in fact, who took the name of Poland and interpreted it in Hebrew as *Polin,* suggesting the phrase "Here shall ye dwell." But in the end this land held no place for them to dwell and therefore no place for God to dwell.

What is inflicted upon the Jews is inflicted upon God, as Judah Halevi once said, and here the Holy One Himself was turned over to the death camps. The capacity to dwell is to be found only within a loving relation to God that finds its expression in the midst of human relation. Once the Jews were refused a place to dwell, they became *other* because they came to signify the homelessness of the others, of the non-Jews. Thus from the question that the Jews put to themselves comes the question put to all: Where are you? Rather than answer, there were those who destroyed the ones who asked.

In Erets Yisrael every Jew has not only a haven but a home, a land in which to dwell, for it is a place where, despite and because of the Jews themselves, God has a place to dwell. In the Land of Israel, however, the difficulty goes to another level. There the question is whether dwelling in the land is to entail a dwelling in God. It is not enough to study God; if God is to be God, then He must be lived.

And if that is to be realized, then the Jews of Israel—indeed, the Jews of the world—are faced with a perhaps insurmountable difficulty. For if that is to be realized, they must be careful not to make Israel into a land that holds no place for the *other*. I think this is why God is so insistent that we treat the stranger in our midst as one of our own. Jews, who were made into strangers in Poland, who were made into the Homeless Ones, must not allow any persons to feel homeless in their own homeland. Otherwise, even in the heart of Israel, they too will be without a home.

This idea, of course, is as old as the Torah and is revealed in the Torah: let your experience as strangers in the land of Egypt—in the land of Poland—teach you something about how to treat the stranger who lives with you in the Promised Land. Do not allow yourselves to come to resemble those who made you homeless in their midst. For if you do, you will have no homeland but only territory.

Then you do not dwell in the Holy One who is *Ha-Makom*, but you lose yourself to a vain struggle for survival that ends by justifying places like Treblinka and Majdanek. I am forever amazed and saddened by the eagerness of so many of us Jews to imitate the ways of those who sent our mothers and fathers to the gas chambers. We imitate them not just in our treatment of others but in the way of life we pursue, in the idols we worship, the success we covet, and the fads we pursue. And I ask myself: did the Nazis win after all?

In Israel I don't have to feel uneasy about being recognized as a Jew, the way I experience that sensation here in Poland. In Israel I encounter another problem, another side of my soul: there I must guard against making the *other human being* feel uneasy for not being a Jew. The creation of a homeland for the Jews in Israel will continue to be impossible as long as there are Jews who live by shouting, "Death to the *other*!" There can be no life for those who cry out for death.

Among some of the "religious" fanatics there are even
those who have shouted to Jews demonstrating for peace,
"You should have died in the ovens at Auschwitz!" How
one Jew could ever say this to another, no matter what
their differences, I shall never understand. Such Jews—if,
indeed, they can be called Jews—end by living on the
blood of their brothers, relishing the hatred that stirs
every time bloodshed fuels their self-serving cause. But, by
the grace of the Holy One, blessed be He, there are some
Jews in Israel who know this and who therefore know what
it means to be a Jew, even if a few of their fellow Jews do
not know.

What troubles me is this: knowing of such places as Treblinka and Majdanek, how can there be anyone, Jewish or
otherwise, who would desecrate these ashes by refusing or
failing to hear the message that cries out from their fath-
omless depths? If Israel can become a land where every
man calls the other his brother, where God comes to life
in the midst of human life, and where, therefore, every
human being might be able to dwell—then it may be said
that Israel arose *in spite of* the Holocaust. But if it turns into
a place where the struggle is not for a dwelling place but
for territory, where one human being is pitted against
another, and where the land is ruled by power rather than
by truth—then it must be said that Israel arose *because of*
the Holocaust.

Today I shall attempt to go to Cracow and from there,
tomorrow, to Auschwitz-Birkenau.

※

On the Train to Cracow

I think I am sitting on the train to Cracow, setting out
once more without knowing where I go. Indeed, do I know

where I have been? This trip has been an intense combination of movements from the spot and movements at the spot, movement every hour, and at every turn a new movement, another shift in the axis of my soul.

The Cracow Express, as I believe it is called, passes through Radom, a town where some of my wife's family once lived. She is ever with me, like the precious treasure of which Rambam speaks. I pray that she and my little girls are well. Please, God, let them be well.

People come aboard this 6:30 train and immediately fall asleep. Those who do not sleep take out some food to eat. Whenever someone speaks to me, I reply in Russian, politely and apologetically, "Please forgive me, but I do not understand."

Please forgive me.

§

Cracow, 16 May 1991

After a six-hour train ride and a thirty-minute cab ride, I am sitting in my room at the Cracow Holiday Inn. From a building called Holy Day I shall make my way to the Planet Auschwitz, or rather to what remains of that Planet.

I hired an independent cab driver, an elderly man who gave me an abbreviated tour of the city. He immediately spotted me as an American and asked if I spoke German; when I replied, "Yes, a little," that was good enough for him. His German wasn't bad, in fact. Like many, many other Poles, he explained, he was out of work and had to live on what came to about ninety dollars per month. He has five children, all grown and married, so at least he did not have to worry about supporting them too.

We drove by shops, and he boasted that all of them were now private businesses. We drove by the local prison, and he declared that it was waiting for the communists.

Here those who were prisoners cannot wait to become jail keepers. Listening to him, I was struck by the truth of the saying that, ultimately and often unwittingly, we come to resemble what we hate. Thus we are punished for our hatred.

Once again, a day that began with some traces of sunshine has grown overcast, gray. Like the gray clothing that so many of the Poles wear, it clothes the land itself. I must be quick to add, however, that, with only a couple of exceptions, the Poles have been very hospitable toward me. They, too, in their own way, have endured terrible suffering. Seeing the life they are faced with, I feel rather sorry for them. Their economy is in critical condition—not as bad as what I saw in Moscow a year ago, but, nonetheless, it is extremely hard for them. And, unlike the Russians, they are surrounded by concentration camp sites. It has to take its toll.

I am very weary. Haven't slept much over the past few days. The intensity of this place is staggering. Still, I must go on. I must keep watch. For the children. For the ashes.

I have already made arrangements to go to Auschwitz-Birkenau tomorrow. There is a bus that leaves from the hotel at 9:30 in the morning, complete with a guide. I have my doubts about the wisdom of this arrangement, but it seems to be the most efficient way to get from here to there.

Right now I am struggling to catch my breath, clutching at my *ruach*, gasping and grasping, trying to take hold of the spirit that forever eludes me. It brings to mind a wrestling match that I once had many years ago. Halfway through the third period of a close battle, my lungs were laboring in what felt like a vacuum and my muscles ached with exhaustion. The temptation to give up was overpowering. Defeat seemed to taste so sweet.

Yes, that is the difficulty: defeat tastes sweeter than victory. Death is not only painless but is actually soothing.

And so we squander our lives in pursuit of the slices of death that come in various forms of sleep and diversion. Look at the life and limb poured into the traffic of drugs, both legal and illicit. Look at the formulas for success: they are all prescriptions for soporifics that transform us into people who sleepwalk through life, deaf to the outcries of children and old men.

And so I beat my head and my heart against the wall of the question: How can the world be what it is after Auschwitz? How can so many of Israel's children have been laid on that terrible altar and neither God nor man receive the offering? How can it all have been to no end? Or to any end? Why are the children still hungry, still broken, beaten, and burned? Why are so many—indeed, all of humanity—still homeless? That is what has happened: when the Jews were forced from their homes and sent to the ovens, humankind was made homeless, all the world made into a wilderness in which we have wandered ever since, with no hope of ever arriving in the Promised Land.

Auschwitz signifies the revocation of the Promise, the impossibility of any promise, because the word Auschwitz means the death of the word, the flight of all meaning from the word. And when the word becomes meaningless, men and women and children become homeless. That interior has been lost inside the crematorium. The homelessness of the Jews is the homelessness of all people. That is why Israel is so precious. It is not only the last haven of the Jews but the last hope of humankind. The Land of Israel is a category, the category according to which the homelessness of humanity is decided.

I think I know now why these tears insist on rising to my nearsighted eyes, why they insist on rising in silence. I think I know now why I weep at the sight of these places: it is not only over what was but over what is and what is yet to be. And the lines from a poem by Judah Halevi return to me:

Between me and thee roar the waves of a sea of tears
And I cannot pass over unto thee.

It seems that we cannot escape from the shadows cast
by the chimneys, the shadows that appear to darken even
the light of God. In the beginning God said, "Let there be
light." In the end that came with Auschwitz man declared,
"Let there be darkness." The first was created through the
word. The latter was brought about through wordlessness.

And yet—thank God for this *and yet*—I continue to
wrap myself each morning in His light as I wind the *talit*
around my body and soul. From the depths of my prayers I
continue to declare, with the Lubavitcher Rebbe,* that the
meaning of creation is couched in the Creator's first utterance: let there be light. Be thou a light unto the world!
Turn even darkness into light!

Like a madman whose voice comes both from within
and from beyond, I inwardly shout this injunction to
myself. But then another voice answers: *How?* How can I?
How dare I? And how can I *not?* Responsibility is the key.
Whatever the event, said the Kotzker, *you* are its origin,
you are the one who must answer for it. Is that why I have
made this pilgrimage—to answer for something that far
exceeds my capacity to answer?

If I have learned anything, penetrated anything, in
coming here, it is the abysmal depth of my ignorance and
my impotence. And the depth of my responsibility. Tomorrow I go for yet another lesson, for another lessening of
myself in a collision with more than I can ever comprehend. Perhaps that is why the Holy One, blessed be He,
has brought me here: so that I may be obliterated and thus
find some deeper way of being *for the other,* beginning with
my family, my friends, my students, and my strangers. If I
aspire to be a pilgrim, then my *I,* my ego, has to become
nothing.

---

*Rabbi Menachem Mendel Schneerson (b. 1902) of Brooklyn.

For there is no other way that I can become a Jew. There must be nothing left of that self-affirmation that goes into the sham of selfhood, if I am ever to become a sign of that light of the Beginning which comes *despite me, for another.* I have come—I have been sent—to be wounded and to become the wound that is a being-for-the-other. It has been said that no matter where you touch a Jew, you touch a wound. Why? Because to be a Jew is to be for-the-other. If my collisions with Treblinka and Majdanek have accomplished anything it is this: I have been robbed of my excuses. Now, in my failure to be a Jew, I betray both the living and the dead. I betray my wife, my parents, my little girls, and children who never had a chance to grow out of their shoes.

The child buried beneath the ashes, turned to ash and adrift on the wind, is no more. But the child buried beneath the years abides, if you, Avraham David ben Avraham, do not bury her deeper still beneath the self-serving weight of your petty condemnations.

I am fighting off sleep. I don't want to awaken again at two o'clock in the morning, unable to go back to sleep. And I am fighting off another kind of sleep.

4 *Sivan* 5751

Cracow, 17 May 1991

I WAS ABLE TO SLEEP fairly late this morning—until about 4:30. The bus to Auschwitz leaves in four hours (it is now 5:30).

As I stood and recited the *shacharit* prayers this morning, two voices were engaged in my head, while a third voice, the voice of my soul joined with the Voice of Another, spoke the prayers. We think we pray to God, but that is not precisely the case, since the prayer is itself divine. Each time we speak to God, God speaks to Himself. Judah Halevi puts it very beautifully:

> Lo, upon my heart is a thought from my God;
> Yea, also upon my tongue is an answer from my Lord.

And so we begin the *Amidah* with the words, "Lord, open my lips, and I shall speak Thy praise!" If a prayer is an effort to draw closer to God, then the utterance of the prayer is its own response.

But this time, as I said, other voices invaded the prayer:

> —*The prayers come with a little more difficulty now, don't they?*
> Perhaps.

—It's the ashes, isn't it? The mountain of ashes at Majdanek is getting in the way of the voice from the mountain at Sinai. Isn't it?

Perhaps.

—They were betrayed, the dead. He, the One to *whom you now pray, turned His face from them, from the children who cried out in vain to the Infinite Absence. The One to whom all life gives thanks, as you refer to Him in your prayers, He is the One who remained silent, who fled the* shmei-hashamayim, *the Heaven of heavens, as the most precious of His Chosen were unchosen and turned over to the flames that ascended to an empty sky.*

Why do you still pray to Him?

Why do I persist in my prayers to Him? So that I won't be the one to betray the little ones. It wasn't God who turned His back on His children. It was man who turned away from God in the murder and in the indifference toward the murder of His children. It wasn't God who silently stood by. No, He was the one who cried out from the darkness that swallowed up His Chosen.

Sometimes I think that maybe God is not the all powerful one we take Him for. Sometimes I imagine that He is perhaps as frail and as helpless as a newborn, that if we do not care for Him, nurture Him, and protect Him, then He will die. What is most precious is always most fragile. And so I pray so as not to lose sight of what there is to love and thus fall among the killers and their spectators. I declare myself to be a Jew not to join the victims but to divorce myself from the executioners and to undo the indifferent ones, to rid myself of the indifference within myself.

The Jew is *other* because he signifies the transformation of *difference* into *non-indifference.* For the Jew, there is no slipping away, no excuse. For the Jew, it is not all the same. For the Jew, there is no principle of identity. Dostoevsky was wrong: "twice two equals four" is *not* the principle of death. The principle of death is "zero equals zero," which amounts to "you are you" and "I am I." For the Jew, the I is discovered within the You. There is in truth only one *I*, only One who may say *anochi*, the utterance of I spoken at Sinai. In that single word, Elie Wiesel once noted, are contained all words ever said and yet to be said. And He who is One is encountered in the Six Million.

The sign on the road from the death camp to the Treblinka train stop comes back to me, the sign of the curve that came after the curve. And I see now what the historians are up to: they proceed by looking into their rearview mirror and put out the signs of what has happened after it has passed. And so history—or rather certain methods of history—is opposed to life. In life a sign is normally an indicator of the yet-to-be, a marker that makes present what is *not yet*, what *is* by virtue of its absence and by virtue of its approach. Absence and approach, in fact, go together. We approach only what is not here; that is why words may signify not only what is but also what is needed and is therefore felt in its absence.

In a way, all signs are signs of a curve in the road, of the unanticipated, signs of the approach of what is yet to be revealed, of the twist in the path we had thought to be straight. Even the signs of history. Especially the signs of history. But on the road leading back from the death camp the sign comes after the curve. It comes too late, comes afterward, because there was no way to imagine it beforehand. No one had ever known this kind of curve, this kind of cave-in. The historians put out their markers, but in vain. This signified cannot be contained by any signifier. And so the thing behind us suddenly lurches ahead of us.

Today is Friday, Erev Shabbat. Today I go to Auschwitz-Birkenau, if it is God's will. Today, on the eve of the observance of the Creation, I go to the site of the undoing of Creation. The Midrash tells us that God created and destroyed many worlds before He settled on this one. But I wonder: perhaps this one too was destroyed at Auschwitz and Treblinka and Majdanek, and we have yet to realize it. We haven't come to the sign that signals the curve behind us. The world has failed to notice its own destruction simply because it did not live through it, because it has no soul left, no eyes to see, no ears to hear, no heart to feel. And so even the sign that tries to show itself through the haze of the smoke that rises from the chimneys goes unheeded. It is the sign of the mushroom.

Maimonides reminds us that on Shabbat we observe both the Creation and the liberation from Egypt. What does Egypt signify? The death that lies in our enslavement to various forms of idolatry, to power, to property and prestige, everything opposed to spiritual life. Auschwitz has this much in common with Egypt: it turns the human being into raw material to be fed into a death factory. Again I wonder: have we truly been liberated from Egypt? Yes, the Torah was given at Sinai. But has it yet been received?

Auschwitz on Erev Shabbat. And this Shabbat comes on the eve of Shevuot, the Sixth of Sivan, when we remember and observe the Revelation at Sinai. Normally the cycle that defines the life of the spirit is Creation - Revelation - Redemption - Shabbat - Shevuot -Messianic Age. But in the overturning of sense and sensibility that came with the advent of the Kingdom of Night, the site of the world's destruction was made to precede the time of its Creation. It turns out that the Rabbis were mistaken in their calculation of the ten things that preceded Creation—the name of the Messiah, the Torah, the Temple, the Heavenly Throne, and so on. There was an eleventh: Auschwitz. For only what precedes the Creation can either redeem it or undo it.

No longer is our remembrance and observance of the Sabbath a remembrance and observance of the Creation and the Liberation alone. It is also an attempt at Re-Creation. That is what was sanctified even before the giving of the Torah at Sinai, sanctified before the Creation because the Nameless One, who knows all, knew of this time after Auschwitz, when we would be in need of some way to begin again. And we cannot begin again without the Sabbath. For without the Sabbath, there can be no Shevuot, no Feast of Weeks to draw the Eternal into time; there can be no giving of the Torah, no Revelation, no life.

After all, the injunction to observe the Seventh Day came before the Revelation at Sinai; indeed, it made possible that Revelation. We were blessed with the Sabbath because the Holy One, blessed be He, knew that this time would come when the Sabbath and Shevuot follow not the Creation but the destruction of the world and thus precede a world that is forever yet to be re-created. The Sabbath and Shevuot thus signify our memory of that future which imparts to us a past. For the opposite of the past, as Elie Wiesel has said, is not the future but the absence of a future. Likewise, the opposite of the future is not the past but the absence of a past. Both are needed to constitute a present, or rather a presence, where the *Shechinah*, the Indwelling Presence, may dwell.

Tradition has never been so critical, so urgent, or so threatened by the ways of Egypt. It has nothing to do with the social, nothing to do with the fashions and fads that so many of us cling to in order to "keep up with the times." On the contrary, tradition is the one means we have of keeping up with eternity. It is the locus where time and eternity, the physical and the metaphysical, intersect. Tradition—and the Ark of the Covenant that it bears—is the memory of the future given to us for this time after Auschwitz as the one path of return that remains open to us. It is the only way to get from Auschwitz to Jerusalem.

All the other ways of modernity, the ways of the Enlightenment that turned tolerance into indifference, lead the way to Auschwitz, Treblinka, Majdanek. All the other signs are signs of our homelessness. God is a dwelling place, we are told in the Torah, and only Torah and tradition can create a place for God and man to dwell. Only the Sabbath and Shevuot, only Torah and tradition, only non-indifference and responsibility—each a different way of expressing the same thing—only this can fetch the embers from the ashes. Only this can overcome the rumbling that rolls over the stones of Treblinka and reverberates through the silence of Majdanek.

I had a round-trip ticket to Treblinka, to that place from which there is no round trip. In order to make my return, I had to find a means of travel other than the train that took me there. I had to take up the most ancient means, the means by which I returned to and maintained my contact with the earth: I had to walk. *Lech lechah,* as it was said unto Abraham in the Torah portion that bears that title: walk into thyself.

It was the means by which Our Father Abraham set out for the Promised Land, set out without knowing where he was going. It was the means by which the Israelites undertook their liberation from Egypt and arrived at Sinai. It is the means of returning to the Torah, the traditional means, the means of tradition. "You will speak of it when you sit in your home and when you walk along your path," as we are enjoined in the *Shma.* Walking down that road that cut through the Polish countryside launched me into the exposure and the vulnerability of the Open. Somehow God gave these battered legs and this daunted heart the strength to do it. Indeed, we walk as much with our heart as with our legs.

Right now it seems to me that I have never felt His Presence so strongly. Yes, the Sabbath is approaching, and I pray that I may approach the Sabbath. Feeling Him nigh, I long to be near my wife and children once more. But I have miles to go before that return. What does tradition tell us? That our family is the vessel of the Indwelling Presence, the realm where all dwelling is made possible. Just as the family is the vessel of tradition and and the Divine Presence, so are tradition and the Torah that fosters it the vessel of the family. The divorce, therefore, that disintegrates the family is a divorce from Torah, from tradition, and from God. And so we are told in the Talmud that when a husband and wife divorce, the Altar itself weeps.

It is time for me to go.

§

Auschwitz-Birkenau

It is cool outside today. A light but steady rain is falling. Once again I do not know what to say or where to begin.

Here I find that there is a sadness upon my sadness. This place is not exactly a tourist attraction, but it approaches that, with its shops and its dining area (yes! a *dining area* on this site where starvation claimed tens of thousands!). The area covered by the concentration camp Auschwitz is much smaller than the huge camp of Birkenau located two kilometers from it. But its parking lot is much larger, large enough to be crowded with dozens of cars and tour buses. A number of those buses have brought school children to see this site; they are all adolescents, since no one under thirteen is admitted to these grounds.

My guide, a very kind woman whose Polish name I cannot recall, tells me that every school boy and girl in the country is required to pay a visit to Auschwitz. I have my doubts as to whether that is a good idea. The school children do not know how to be silent. Therefore they do not know how to look upon or listen to this place. My guide, however, does a good job of working around them and the crowds of others who mill about the area. On the other hand, moving through these grounds with a guide, I am unable to be alone with the place. That too is disturbing.

I have to cut through layer upon layer of masks and buffers to get at this thing called Auschwitz, and still it eludes me. I gaze at photograph after photograph; most of them were taken secretly by an SS soldier who sent them back to his wife in Germany. I look long upon them all and try to impose the black and white images upon the scenes around me, upon the blocks, the assembly area, the crematorium, the house where the Camp Commandant Hoess and his family lived under a massive cloud of smoke and a constant drizzle of ash.

My guide reminds me repeatedly that there were no trees or birds here in those terrible days, as there are now. There was no grass, not because it was trampled down but because it was eaten. There was nothing surrounding the brick blocks of Auschwitz that once housed Austrian soldiers except mud and screams and the vicious barking of dogs. I strain to hear those sounds, but the noise from the crowds that surround me drowns them out. And yet there is a faint echo. Enough to make me feel as though I am drowning in it.

Going through the blocks, I collided with terror upon terror. As in Majdanek, there was a room piled to the ceiling with shoes and not far from it a mound of metal-rimmed eyeglasses, enough for the Nazis to collect them and use them as scrap metal. I wonder how many eyeglasses it takes to make a tank. I wonder how many tanks were made from the eyeglasses of Auschwitz. Perhaps the only way to try to see this place is through those eyeglasses, and the only way to walk through this place is through those shoes.

And so I looked and walked and came to the room piled high with every kind of brush and then to the room with the mountain of suitcases bearing the names of their dead owners. Then there were the stacks of crutches and artificial limbs taken from the first to be selected for death, prosthetic devices taken from children by men with prosthetic souls. And there was the hair… a room piled to the ceiling with hair, every strand of it discolored by the gas into a nondescript gray, all differences collapsed into a single shade that resembled the sky overhead, all difference transformed into indifference. The hair was shaved from the heads of the bodies and used to make cloth and clothing, SS uniforms. Another instance of the impossible made possible: human beings covered themselves with clothing made from human hair!

Against my will I pictured an SS man wearing an outfit of Jewish hair, herding Jewish men, Jewish women, Jewish children down the steps that traced their last steps and into the gas chambers. In Birkenau the gas chambers are underground, like vast graves, where human beings were ushered in and dragged out, so that they might be raised up through the chimneys and sent to heaven only to settle again over the face of the earth. Their ashes, tons of ashes, were dumped into surrounding ponds and scattered over nearby fields. The death camp Birkenau still has that faint odor of death about it. Although I know that I have never been here before, the odor *reminds* me of something from a past not my own, a past that tries to become some small part of my present.

As for the smell of the human life that was crushed on this site, it is strongest in the empty wooden blocks that remain standing in Birkenau next to the forest of chimneys where the other wooden blocks had stood, warehouses that stored the human raw material waiting to be processed in the furnaces.

Across the tracks that lead into the camp, opposite the place where Jews were unloaded from the trains and the initial selections were conducted, stand rows of blocks made of brick. The bricks in those blocks once formed the dwelling places of the village of Birkenau. Himmler stood on a bridge that spans the railroad tracks along the road from Auschwitz to Birkenau and ordered the village to be dismantled brick by brick, so that the first structures of yet another death camp could be erected. Auschwitz, you see, soon proved to be too small to handle the task of extermination. "Remember this bridge," my guide told me, and once again I thought of the passage from the Talmud: judgment occurs on a bridge.

I realized that there is no more stark representation of the homelessness of humanity than this: bricks that had been used to build dwelling places were turned into structures of death, spaces opposed to all human dwelling. Homes were made into prisons, people into commodities, men into animals, God into ash. A community was disintegrated in order to erect the archetype of disintegration.

It brings me back to the eternal difficulty of dwelling. Auschwitz-Birkenau is precisely the opposite of a dwelling place. It is the dwelling place dismantled, the logical outcome of exile. One Birkenau was taken apart and another was assembled. The home was made into homelessness, houses into blocks, hearths into crematoria. As I stood in the empty wooden blocks of Birkenau, stared at the empty plank beds, and breathed in the odor of ghostly human remains, I think I felt closer to this place that when I was surrounded by the exhibits of the concentration camp Auschwitz. There are no exhibits in Birkenau. Only emptiness. Only the void.

There was, however, one hallway in one of the blocks of Auschwitz. It was lined with the faces of prisoners photographed during the first two years of the camp's operation, with the date of their entry and the date of their death inscribed under each photo, as if those dates were essential to their identity. And in their eyes, Jewish eyes filled with the terror of men who no longer understood anything, was inscribed my name. As I filed past them, those eyes reached out at me like invisible hands and clawed their way into my own eyes, like the eyes of the Angel of Death, the Angel with a Thousand Eyes. I tried to

look away, but I could not. I tried to look at these grim sur-
roundings through those eyes, but I could not. I could
only gape with impotence and shame.

I saw another photograph. It was in the Jewish Pavilion,
where there is a hole cut into the floor to reveal Jewish
gravestones driven into this earth that is itself one massive
grave. The photograph pictured a man wearing *talit* and
tefillin who, more powerfully than any image I have ever
seen, resembled...Jesus. Looking into that picture, it occurred to me that if, indeed, that young Hasid from Nazareth had been resurrected from the dead, he was sent
back to his death, along with his brothers, here in this
place which surpasses everything that Golgotha could
have been.

Still, the talk was too much, the markers too many.
They hid what they were supposed to reveal, obscured
what they were intended to clarify. The camp is covered
not only with leaves of grass and the veil of time but with
talk and signs that cannot convey what they struggle to signify.

Yes, I passed under the passageway over which was written *Arbeit Macht Frei*. I walked a short distance along the
track in Birkenau where Jews were unloaded and sent to
their deaths. I passed through the gas chamber in the
Auschwitz crematorium and gazed and gawked at the pun-
ishment cells in Block Eleven, the Death Block. But I was
never there. Or is it that the camp isn't here but somewhere else? Can it be that the dead carried it off with
them, carried it up the chimneys and into the heavens to
confront the Creator with this overturning of Creation?
Or is it buried beneath this soil made of Jewish loam?
They had no cemeteries, as Wiesel has pointed out: we are
their cemeteries.

Auschwitz is tucked away in the beautifully forested
hills of the Polish countryside. On the way here we passed
by quaint villages, cottages with thatched roofs, lovely

churches. And then we came to the gate inscribed with *Arbeit Macht Frei*, a place insanely out of place. Like the orchestra situated at the gate where it played as prisoners marched out to work each morning and then lumbered back at nightfall, their dead slung over their backs. The bodies swayed in time with Mozart, insanely out of time and place like the world that has lost its place and its meaning, like all of humanity that no longer has a place, like the Place Himself who disappeared on the Highway to Heaven.

Or is it rather that the orchestra is not out of place, but this *place* itself, everything around it, is out of place. That's it: I have come to a place that is itself out of place. I am here, but the place is not here. Or perhaps this is the place all right, but I…I am elsewhere, stranded in a realm from which I take up this pen and scratch my way through a wall of chit-chat in an effort to get at it. I understand why so many protective barriers are erected here. Who, indeed, can bear to approach the abyss without some kind of guardrail? But there are some things from which we should not be protected.

I don't think I have ever been so frustrated. Auschwitz is packaged in a framework that is so easy to see, so open to seeing, so conducive to sightseeing, that it blinds you to everything you encounter. And yet, beneath the surface of all this artifice there lurks something that even this surface cannot hide.

It comes from above and below, oozing through the blackened ceiling in the crematorium and rising up from the concrete floor where so many fell. It creeps out of the narrow cells in the basement of the Death Block, where four people at a time were forced to stand through the night and through the day, locked into the praying position without respite, until they were either shot or died from standing. And above the basement, down the hall from the SS officer's quarters, it is written on the walls of holding cells, where prisoners in this prison within a prison wrote their last words, never knowing whether other eyes would read them. Yet it is not we who read those words. No, they read us, see through us, and inscribe themselves upon our souls.

Like the Death Block within its walls, Auschwitz is a prison imprisoned within itself.

The Nazis tried to hide it or to dress it behind flower beds and music, and where they failed we have succeeded, despite ourselves. I think that this place should not be so easy to see or even to get to. People should have to walk or crawl here, rather than ride in the comfort of climate-controlled tour buses. Once here, they should be discouraged from entering or frightened away. Dressed as it is, at first you get the impression that there is nothing fearsome about it, no danger of collisions with darkness or of falling into the void. There are too many handrails to hold on to—tour guides and guidebooks, exhibits framed in tinted glass and kept at a safe distance, signposts directing you here and there, everywhere except into the Nowhere that is Auschwitz.

And so we look on and shake our heads, our souls unshaken. But if you pay attention even to these precautions, then soon you realize that all of the trappings are here precisely because of the horror that threatens at every turn to swallow you up.

Gazing at the railroad tracks that led to the site where the Jews were unloaded from the trains, I saw for an instant the onset of night. Suddenly I was an unwilling time traveler caught in that vortex where time was twisted into something else. The floodlights went on, and the air overflowed with the inhuman screaming and shouting of SS men and with the silent terror of Israel's children.

A fat pig who had all but lost any resemblance to a man began pointing this way and that, now to the right, now to the left. Parents were separated from children, brothers from sisters and from one another, their piles of luggage left behind, marked with their names and addresses so that these people who would never come back could find them when they returned. The suitcases that contained the gleanings of a lifetime are still there waiting for them, piled up like inmates in one of the Auschwitz blocks, where the eyes of tourists stare hard at them and hardly comprehend what they behold.

Three camps in fours days. It seems like four years. Or four minutes. I can't tell any more. Time has collapsed around me. Rambam says in the *Guide for the Perplexed* that time is among the first of God's creations. In this place, on this Planet Auschwitz, man managed to uncreate it. Katzetnik's remark comes to mind. He was here not for two years, as he puts it, but for two Auschwitz-years. How many millennia does that translate into?

Time: the train to Warsaw leaves at 6:10 in the morning. On Shabbat. Yes, God forgive me, I shall travel on Shabbat. But when the sun sets tonight I shall leave off with this writing for a day, in observance of the Sabbath. My trip to Warsaw in the morning is another leg of a long journey to Jerusalem via these campsites. I know, however, that this is no excuse for traveling on the Sabbath. After treading these grounds, I have been robbed of all my excuses.

I asked my guide how often she comes here.

"Every day," she said. "But only in May. A month is all I can stand. It's very hard. But somebody has to do it. It's very important."

So tomorrow she will come back here and attempt to explain what cannot be explained. And how shall I explain it to my students from a podium in a classroom at Oklahoma State? Having been here, I suppose I can describe what it all looks like now, how it is laid out, where it is located. But if I cannot penetrate the veils that conceal it even as I stand here, how am I to get those who are so young and innocent to see through the veils five thousand miles from here? I may show them photographs, but how will they understand that what they see in the photographs is not it at all?

There is a group of men standing behind me. They are speaking German. They are laughing. And the place is covered with grass and dandelions.

My soul is reeling at the scream that I hold in my throat.

Shevuot 5751

Warsaw, 19 May 1991

MY SOUL IS STILL bursting with the images, the sounds, and the silences of the last few days. The effort to convey it all becomes increasingly difficult as it becomes increasingly needful. And the more needful it becomes, the more mindful I am of my impotence to tell it.

When I got back to my hotel in Cracow, I noticed that my shoes were caked with bits of dried mud from the grounds of Auschwitz-Birkenau. This, of course, was no ordinary mud. No, it was mud made from the ashes of the dead and the tears of the heavens. I scraped some of it into a piece of paper that I now carry in my pocket. And some of it remains on my shoes, so that I track it wherever I go.

Or rather it tracks me and traces my tracks, following me over the face of the earth, over the pavement of Warsaw, into the Synagogue and about the Ghetto. Those bits of earth and ash now create the path I follow even as I follow it, leaving their mark on the path my feet will travel forever hereafter. Wherever I go the ground will be tainted with the grounds of Auschwitz-Birkenau. It is the dirt I take with me tomorrow, God willing, when I leave for the

Land of Israel. And it will follow me to Jerusalem, all the way to the Western Wall.

I carry in my pocket stones from the other camps. Just as the Jews place pebbles on graves, so do I carry on me stones from those camps, myself a burial site for the dead. For the last five years I have carried with me a stone from Dachau, the one shaped like a petrified tear fallen from the sky—or perhaps like a drop of blood from a bleeding God. Or it may be that God weeps tears of blood, like a woman in Auschwitz I once heard about. She went to the mistress of a Nazi officer to plead for the life of her sister. The mistress agreed, and the life was spared. Years later, when the one who was spared met the mistress and thanked her, the mistress replied, "No, it is not for you to thank me. You see, when your sister came to me she was crying. And her tears…her tears were red. She was weeping tears of blood. It was a sign from God. He is the one you should thank."

To this tear-shaped stone from Dachau I have added stones from Treblinka and from Majdanek, pieces of the ground that crumbled out from under humanity, out from under the Creator of heaven and earth Himself. I took them with me to Auschwitz-Birkenau, these fossilized bits of tears shed by Rachel weeping for her children and refusing to be consoled. Or might they be pieces from the tablets that Moshe Rabbenu* threw to the ground?

In the *Pirke d'Rabbi Eliezer** we are told that the tablets fell from Moshe's hands when the letters of the Ten Utterances flew off them at the sight of the terrible idolatry at the foot of the mountain. As he descended Mount Sinai, says Rabbi Eliezer, the tablets had borne Moshe, not Moshe the tablets. But when the letters saw the abomination and fled the stones, the void they left on the blank

---

*Hebrew for "Our Teacher Moses."

**Biblical commentary attributed to Rabbi Eliezer ben Hyrcanus, a *tanna,* or teacher, of the late first and early second centuries.

tablets became too heavy for him to bear, and they all but crushed him.

Tradition has it, in fact, that there was but a single word uttered at Sinai, the *Anochi* or the *I* of I Am. That is the word that has fled from the bits of stone that I carry in my pocket. And I carry them in order to find some way to return to them the Word that was lost. I carry them to remind myself of what was lost and to warn myself not to become one of those who drive the letters of the *Anochi* from humanity.

Since leaving the site of the death camps Auschwitz-Birkenau, I have carried one more bit of stone in my pocket. Unlike the other stones, however, it is not from the grounds of either Auschwitz or Birkenau. I hesitate to say where it is from. But as soon as I hesitate, I know that I must go on. It is a small, pea-sized chip from the concrete wall of the gas chamber in the Auschwitz crematorium. As I traced my fingers along the wall of the passageway leading from the gas chamber to the ovens, it fell into my hand as though placed there by the hand of Another.

My whole body trembles each time I touch it. For it is permeated with the unheard screams and the deafening silences of God's chosen. At first I did not know what to do with it, whether to throw it to the ground or receive it as it was offered. It is not like the other stones, no, not like those retrieved from an open ground under a silent, sunlit sky. It is a piece of a wall of darkness that shut out all life, all light, all words, a wall fashioned by human hands bent on the murder of humanity, of meaning, of God. As it was placed into my hand, so I held it in my hand.

The next day, yesterday, I was riding the six-o'clock train back to Warsaw. A lovely little girl sat across from me. Gazing at my foreign, bearded face, she snuggled closer to her mother, and within me there arose a painful longing to be with my own little girls, to return to my wife and... and then, ever so faintly, the piece of the wall that I bore in my pocket spoke to me.

As though announcing its name, or calling my own, it said, "The Wall."

My hand went into my pocket to take hold of it, and suddenly I knew why it had been entrusted to me and what I must do with it: I must take it to the Western Wall in Jerusalem and insert it into the cracks of that Wall, along with the thousands of folded bits of paper inscribed with prayers and slipped into the Wall so that they might be closer to the ear of God.

On those crumpled shreds of paper are written the deepest longings, the most sublime supplications of the world, rendered in all the languages of the world. There are no words, however, on this piece of stone. Just the silence of all words, the silence that surpasses all languages. Every prayer, every outcry, raised up and fallen silent in that gas chamber will finally find its way to the ear of the Holy One to whom they were addressed. Those wails will finally be taken to the Wailing Wall and made part of the eternal wailing that rises up from the very stones in the Wall. This bit of stone will be a link between a wall of death and the Wall of life, between a wall that closed over the children of Israel like a tomb of darkness and the Wall that does not close off but opens up the light that brings life to the world. One was a barrier between God and man, while the other has always been a portal to the two, for the two. I must make this piece of stone into part of the passageway that returns man to God, to his fellow man, and to himself.

But then, in a moment of cowardice, doubts rose up within me: Could I be hearing things? Was it the Evil One tempting me with the defilement of a holy site? Would the meeting of these two walls amount to a desecration of the Western Wall?

For a time I was not sure of the answers to these questions that followed in the wake of the voice. But finally I answered: No. I have heard the voice. These two walls are linked each to the other, just as both are tied to Sinai. Without this linkage, the wall of the gas chamber in the crematorium would remain the place where Jewish history, Jewish presence, and with it the history of humanity, came to an end. But it does not end there. Despite all appearances, despite the temptation to suppose otherwise, the victory did not go to the SS. I do not know that it went to anyone. But it did not go to the SS.

Having determined what I must do with the relic I carried with me—not only to make this linkage but to become a link—I realized that I had never before understood the full meaning of the phrase that appears on so many of these memorial sites: Never Again. The point in studying the history of the Churban,* I realized, is not to keep it from happening again. Indeed, those who perpetrate atrocity are often well acquainted with the history of atrocity; Hitler, for example, studied thoroughly the history of the Armenian genocide. No, the point is to confront those questions that familiarize us not only with *what was* but with *what is* and with *who we are.*

The declaration of "Never Again," therefore, is not the drawing of a barrier but the creation of a linkage. Its aim is not just the prevention of one thing but the nurturing and creation of something else, not a negation but an affirmation. If the meaning of "Never Again" is only negative, then we negate ourselves with its utterance. Worse than that, as a consequence of that, we end up negating others, and soon we hear ourselves crying out, "Death to…!" Is that the meaning of "Never Again"? No. God spare us from making it into that. The survivors may have declared, "Never Again," but, miraculously, they generally did not seek vengeance. Justice perhaps, if that is possible,

*Yiddish term for the Holocaust, from the Hebrew word meaning "destruction."

but not vengeance. There is a difference.

If we are to restore meaning to the word and thus to life, then we must seek a meaning in this *never* that is an affirmation of life, both for a people and for the single human being. And so it strikes me that this "Never Again" means not only *"never again* shall we allow this to happen"—as if the Jews allowed it to happen in the first place—but *"never again* shall *I* do or say anything that plays into the negation of life."

This "Never Again" is not directed toward others but rather is addressed to me in my responsibility to and for others. Never again shall I be cruel, thoughtless, condemning, self-serving, indifferent, irresponsible, deaf and blind. And *always* shall I strive to dwell in the House of *HaShem.* Which means, always shall I be thankful, always shall I be thoughtful, always shall I rejoice, love, embrace my wife and children, be a witness to my students, be present before my family and friends, and take on those characteristics without which, according to the Talmud, a Jew is not a Jew: modesty, generosity, and lovingkindness.

"Never Again" has to amount to this "Always" if it is to mean anything and if anything is to have meaning. Failing to generate this meaning, we betray the dead. We slay them yet again and thus become accomplices to their murder. So let us remember and observe, not simply to prevent a repetition of the past, as the cliché goes, but to bring about the advent of the future and to establish some substance within the present. Let us remember not only what was but who we *are,* before whom we stand, to whom we are called to answer, and what is entrusted to us. Let us remember so that we do not die and do not murder in yet another shout of "Death to..." anyone. For this fatal cry is the mold that casts us in the image of the enemy. Let us remember so that we may live in the affirmation of the dearness of life, in the embrace of *the other human being,* that makes us who we are.

Yesterday, on Shabbat, I arrived here in Warsaw by nine in the morning, and by ten I was sitting in the synagogue. The hours I spent there, though quite different, were as moving as the hours I spent in the camps. In the camps I saw the places where the reign of death had reached its height. But there, in the Warsaw Synagogue, I was in the midst of life's essence. I began to sense the meaning of the traditional saying that on the Sabbath every Jew is instilled with a second soul, for I could feel the soul of the Sabbath merging with my own.

The cantor's voice was beautiful, courageous, overflowing with faith and thanksgiving. In every word, with each intonation, he conveyed the history of a people and the miracle of the remnant that the Jew signifies. Feeling simultaneously out of place and finally in place, I quietly joined a company of about fifty men seated at benches with book stands made for prayer and study. Most were clean shaven, but a few looked as if they had just stepped out of the 1930s, complete with the beards and the dress of Polish Jews. I marveled at how stubbornly this stiff-necked people continues with life and with a defiant affirmation of life. And I prayed that I might one day be worthy of belonging to them.

As the prayers rose up, the women looked on from the balcony, like angels from on high, and I understood that this was precisely the proper arrangement for the worship of God, with each human being in his or her rightful place. I realized what was lost in the mingling of the sexes in synagogues all over the world. I realized that this collapse of difference in the name of social equality led to a certain indifference toward the holy, without which there can be no social freedom. This arrangement within the sanctity of the synagogue has nothing to do with the issues of social equality or inequality. It concerns not the scheme of life in the world of business and society but the origin of life from above. It belongs not to the social but to the sacred, a structure that declares the mystery and the sanctity of life, an order that reveals the mission of each man and woman in life.

The women are elevated above the men as if they were ushering the words of the prayers higher still, sending them on their way to the Heaven of heavens, beyond the confines of the synagogue. Their elevation above the men is indicative of a purity that women enjoy in their proximity to life's origins, and it suggests why we are told in the Talmud that he who handles the Holy Scrolls is thereby made unclean. Is it not from a position of absence and therefore from a kind of impurity that we come to the Torah in search of truth and holiness? A man handles the Scrolls precisely because he is unclean, because he is more distant from the Giver of Life: no man ever bore a child.

Sitting there, looking upon those faces gazing down upon the men, I recalled what Avigdor said to the woman who would be a man, near the end of the film *Yentl*. "Why do you want to study the mysteries?" he asked her. "You *are* the mystery!"

Tradition tells us that when God gave the Torah at Sinai, the women (the House of Jacob) had to accept it before the men (the House of Israel) could accept it. And, according to the Midrash, God liberated the Israelites from Egypt for four reasons: the Hebrews did not change their names, they did not give up their language, they did not reveal their secrets, and...their women remained chaste. In the hands of the Jewish women, therefore, lie the sanctity and the salvation of the Jewish people. Yes, the arrangement of the women above and the men below made more sense to me—it was a much deeper sign of the higher relation—than the mixed seating in the lounge chairs that I have known in other synagogues.

When the Torah Scrolls were taken out of the Ark and the old Rabbi began to read, I could no longer hold back my tears. According to the rules of logic and reason, according to everything I had seen in Poland, what I was witnessing should not be taking place. Only God could have brought this about. Only God could have gathered together this remnant that included Jews not only from Poland but from all over the world. This land was once a center of Jewish life, perhaps *the* center of Jewish spirituality in the world. And, perhaps, in a way, it still is. Never before have I felt so close to a Center, so close to a Presence that defied and thus transcended the logic of the world, as when I sat in the Warsaw Synagogue and listened to the Rabbi chant the Torah portion.

The reading this week, as always on the Sabbath prior to Shevuot, was *Bemidbar*, which means "In the Wilderness." Indeed, these Jews came together in this synagogue like a pillar of fire, gathered by a terrible pillar of consuming fire, in the heart of a wilderness. Nearly all of the men assembled there were over sixty years old, old enough to harbor a memory of those days when synagogues all over Europe were filled with Jews and set aflame. What will become of these Torah Scrolls forty years hence?

After the service we all went to an annex for *Kiddush*.* There I was invited to sit with a man and his wife and their son. Mr. Blum, as he introduced himself, was close to seventy years old. His wife's name was Erika, and their son, who was no more than thirty, was called by my own name, David. The three of them spoke Yiddish among themselves, most of which I could pick up. David, in fact, was on his way to Columbia University to spend the summer studying Yiddish literature—another miracle.

Mr. Blum explained to me that he had brought David from their home in Melbourne to show him the places where his father had spent his childhood in what had been the Jewish neighborhood of Warsaw. He had fled the city on 7 September 1939, one week after the Nazi invasion of Poland, and set off with some four hundred thousand

---

*A blessing said over wine after the Saturday morning service.

other Jews toward the East, where he spent the war years in Siberia. In 1945 he managed to return to Warsaw, a city that was almost completely destroyed, and in 1946 he left for good, perhaps because the Jewish population of Poland had been reduced from over three and a half million to less than three thousand.

"I brought my son here to show him my home," Mr. Blum explained to me. "But, of course, it is no more."

Once again I was colliding with the problem of homelessness and what it means. In this old man, it occurred to me, the sum of humanity was gathered, the whole of a humanity seeking a home that is no more, trying to impart to their children something of what no longer stands. "I used to swim in the Vistula," my guide at Auschwitz told me. "But no more. Now it is polluted, poisoned." Yes, poisoned. A poisoned earth with poisoned water can harbor no place for its inhabitants to dwell. People struggle to retrieve some shred of their childhood that they may offer to their children, but in vain. And if their childhood is lost, then so is the childhood of their children.

In the Midrash we are told that when God was about to give the Torah to the Israelites gathered at Sinai, He asked them what they would put up as a kind of collateral, to assure that they would take good care of the gift they were about to receive.

"We offer You the Patriarchs," they said, "our forefathers, whose deeds are beyond reproach."

But God refused, saying, "No, they are already in My debt."

"We offer You the Prophets," they answered, "those chosen to bear Your Holy Word."

"No," God again refused. "They too have their own debt to pay."

Finally, the Israelites cried out in a single voice, "We offer You our children."

And God spoke to the infants at their mothers' breasts

and to the embryos in their mothers' wombs, asking them, "Do you agree to stand as surety for the Torah I am about to give?"

And in a single voice, they answered, "Yes, we agree."

So in our preservation and protection of the Torah, of the Tree of Life entrusted to us, there is far more than our own lives at stake. We receive what comes to us from the Holy One, blessed be He, only as we pass it on to our children. And if we should lose what has been placed in our care, our children are themselves lost, generation upon generation.

Mr. Blum had brought his child to Warsaw in order to pass on to him some invisible remnants of his own lost childhood. Why? So that his child might have a childhood to pass on to his own children, so that his child might not be lost. First he took him to the Warsaw Synagogue to hear the reading of the Torah. Then he would take him to the Warsaw Ghetto and to those areas of the city where the Torah that had been the basis of life was consumed.

Then yet another miracle came my way: Mr. Blum asked me if I would like to join him and his son for a walk through "the old neighborhood." I gratefully accepted the invitation, and after *Kiddush* Mr. Blum, his son, and I set off. Mrs. Blum, who was very tired, went back to their hotel not far from the synagogue.

We began by taking a bus into the heart of what had been the Warsaw Ghetto, where we got off on a street named for the inventor of Esperanto, L. L. Zamenhof. Here—where the words and the meanings of all languages had been starved to death, where people had been isolated from humanity to be rounded up for deportation to the gas chambers, where the dead lay in this very street—here was this street named for the man who sought a language and a life that could be shared by all people. Now this street, like most of the other streets of the Ghetto, is lined with apartment buildings. Thousands live on this site where not so long ago life had been made impossible for thousands. I reeled at the irony. It is no wonder that the divisions within the land of Poland run so deep.

From there we set out on foot, David and I hurrying to keep up with his father. We walked and walked, until I grew amazed at the stamina of this old man who looked so small, so frail. Then I remembered that this was a man who walked to Russia and back, who had survived nearly six years in Siberia, and who knew enough about life to bring his son to this site. Very soon I realized that a great force, the force of memory, was driving him. With every step he groped for a past that eluded him, and soon his movements took on an air of desperation. And desperation, like memory, is also a tremendous force. At times all but running, he hurried to note now the name of this street, now the name of that, seeking the signs that would tell him where he was and what to pass on to his son.

"The Poles have restored the prewar names of the streets," he explained, somewhat frustrated. "But they have arranged them in a different order."

Yes, I thought, it is all in a different order, all *on* a different order, an order that is disorder. The names, like all the other words of the language, are confused, disarrayed, disconnected from the places they struggle to signify. The names would not lead this old man back to the home where he grew up. In order to get there he needed something other than these names out of place, something more than a language that loses what it would convey in the very effort to speak. He needed the words and the silence of memory.

From the heart of the Ghetto Mr. Blum took us to the Pawiak Prison, that infamous fortress where the Nazis tortured and murdered Jews and non-Jews alike. He used to walk past it, he said, on his way to school. I wondered what sounds he might have heard coming from beyond those walls, but I was afraid to ask. Just outside the entrance to the prison stands an old, dead tree. It is covered with small placards bearing the names of some of those who perished there, the only traces that remain of those brave lives. More names out of place, I thought, more signs out of joint. Towering over the entrance to this place, the tree with its names brought to mind the Tree of Knowledge of Good and Evil. On the day you eat this fruit.... Or was it a Tree of Life transformed into a Tree of Death?

From there we went to the memorial erected on the site of the Warsaw Ghetto Uprising, the first civilian uprising of the war, organized in April 1943 by the Jews who were trapped here. The faces, the bodies, the figures carved on one side of the Memorial emanated immense strength and resolve, and on the other side—immense sadness. I have never seen exile—the exile of a people, of humanity, of the Word itself—so powerfully sculpted. The memorial portrays a procession of the Jews driven from their homes by the SS. The central figure is reminiscent of Moses himself, cradling the Torah Scrolls that alone held out any hope of preserving an ember of life from the flames that were about to consume them.

It was not gold or possessions that they bore as they fled but the Truth of Torah, which is the breath of God and the essence of the Jew. These Jews were forced from their homes by the minions of homelessness, yet with them they carried the Place, *HaMakom,* embodied in the Torah Scrolls. Those who bear the Ark of the Covenant, I recalled the passage from the Midrash, are borne by it. And I remembered a statement made by Rabbi Haninah ben Teradion,* when his daughter wept for the Torah Scrolls that were to be burned at the stake with him: The Torah is made of fire, and fire cannot burn fire.

And then it hit me: What was being forced into the exile portrayed on the Memorial was not just one commu-

---

*A *tanna* of the early second century, martyred by the Romans.

nity among others but the Holy One Himself, the Indwelling Presence that makes any and all dwelling possible. This memorial to the Jews, therefore, was a memorial to the homelessness of all humanity. And I encountered it, or collided with it, on the Sabbath known as *Bemidbar,* on the eve of the Sixth of Sivan, the day when the Torah was given to humanity so that humanity might have a place to dwell, given but yet to be received.

Why was the Torah revealed at Mount Sinai, outside of the Promised Land? According to the Midrash, it was so that the Jews would not be so conceited as to think that it was theirs alone nor the Gentiles so complacent as to think that it did not apply to them. Yes, these images of exile and uprising carved into the Memorial summon the memory not of the Jews alone.

And trailing along behind the sculpted procession of Israel's children going into exile came Mr. Blum, searching for the place where his home had stood, so that he could show it to his child. And behind Mr. Blum, his son and myself. On he went, down the streets that led back into the Jewish neighborhood where now there are no Jews, back into a memory that threatened to slip through his fingers.

"I'll know it by the park," he said, as much to reassure himself as to inform his son and me. "There was a park around here somewhere. It *has* to be here. And across from it was my house. But the names on the streets, the names and the numbers, they're out of place."

Yes, out of place ever since names were turned into numbers. A memory and a name, *yad vashem,* that's what he was after. But the sign was lost. No signs. And yet...

We walked further and then we walked some more, David and I hurriedly stepping up our pace to keep up with his father. Now and then the old man stopped to ask a passerby for directions, and then he would move on. Finally we came to the park, and Mr. Blum's face lit up at the discovery. Yes, it was there, just as he had said. He had not been dreaming. See it? There it is! And across from the park...a building.

It was surrounded with an iron fence, and at the iron gate that closed off the walkway to the building stood an armed guard. For some reason the prohibition against laying iron on the stones of the Altar went through my mind. There was no getting past this fence. It stood there as immovable as the fence of time and destruction that invisibly surrounded the site, forever cutting this old man off from the place where he had been a child, with a mother and a father who loved him and protected him until...

Mr. Blum, his son, and I pressed against the fence to try to read the sign on the building that stood on the other side. Suddenly he cried out in disbelief, "It's the Embassy of the People's Republic of China! This house of slavery has taken the place of my home!" He gazed at me in disbelief, as if I might be the one who could explain the unexplainable.

Indeed, there could be nothing more opposed to the Jewish presence that once graced this site than this edifice that housed murderers who were there to maintain good relations with the world. Not only did Mr. Blum fail to find any trace of the familial and the familiar, but he encountered what was for him the image of estrangement itself. Did he regret having brought his son all the way from Australia only to see this profanity? I don't think so. Even in this terrible discovery there was an important lesson to be learned about the frailty and the dearness of home and childhood. Nonetheless I ached for him. And in my eyes was the reflection of the tears that rose up in his.

On a corner not far from the Embassy stands the National Library of Poland, the repository of all Polish knowledge. But all the knowledge housed within those towering walls does not amount to even a fraction of what Mr. Blum knows all too well, of what he would rather not know.

We walked on, past the National Library. I followed Mr. Blum and his son, not knowing where he was taking us now. Perhaps he had decided that this could not be the place where his home had stood, that it must be somewhere else. Or at least his childhood must be somewhere else. We turned up Dluga Street and came to an abrupt halt at a building that had survived the war. With a faint, nostalgic smile, Mr. Blum announced that in this building there used to be a cinema where he and his friends would go each week.

"Everything I knew about the world," he said, "I got from the newsreels I saw here."

I wondered what he saw in 1939.

Proceeding west on Dluga, we passed the Economics Faculty of the University of Warsaw. Next to it stood another structure that had survived the war. Mr. Blum told us that from this building twenty-five prisoners destined for Pawiak were rescued from the Gestapo by Jewish resistance fighters. He explained that before the war this two-story building had been six stories high and that here the Jewish Socialists used to hold their meetings and lay their plans for a brave new world.

"Those were exciting days," he added. "The air was alive with new hopes and new ideas. All lost."

From there we headed back toward the north. I could see that Mr. Blum was still determined to find some shred of some signifier of a time when he called this place home. He was like a man running about in a dream—or a nightmare—of home, in which he knows this must be home, yet he recognizes nothing. Pressing on, we soon entered the park that we had passed on the way to the site where the Chinese Embassy now stands. And then, like men coming upon an oasis in a desert, we arrived at an old stone gateway that had been there from the time of Mr. Blum's childhood. The old man paused to drink in the sight, and his face beamed at last with recognition.

As we walked through that gate, we stepped into another time, or into some remnant of a time, when dwelling in the world was still possible, when the names of the streets were in their proper place and a Jewish home stood across the lane. It seemed a miracle that to the left there was still the small hill where Mr. Blum and his playmates would spend short winter days riding their sleds. On the right was the pond where they used to ice skate.

"I had thought it would be much bigger," the old gentleman commented on the size of the pond.

"No," his son answered. "You were much smaller."

The mound of earth, the little body of water, the stone gateway—they added up to the sum of a childhood that ended on 7 September 1939.

A line from the *Shma* came to me: "You will inscribe it on your doorposts and on your gates." The doorpost that had held the *mezuzah* that had made this man's house into a home had long since been turned to dust and ash. But the gate of stone was still there. And I felt that on its posts there should be a *mezuzah*. As it was, this stone threshold was more a *matzeva* than anything else, a blank tombstone marking the burial site of an old man's childhood. I had an urge to hold him in my arms the way I hold my babies and tell him that everything is all right. But everything is not all right. Nothing is all right.

From the park we went to one more site where Mr. Blum spent his boyhood years. This trek took us through narrow byways and long alleys, until we came at last to a large circular courtyard. On one side of the courtyard stood a dwelling where, according to Mr. Blum, the Bund once had its headquarters. On the other was an apartment house where there used to live the girl who had been Mr. Blum's childhood sweetheart.

He told us that she had spent the war years in the south, working as a servant for some Italian officers. When the war ended, she returned to Warsaw. Since she was one of the few people in Poland who could speak Italian, she immediately got a job in the Italian Embassy. There she met the man whom she was to marry. He later became one of the most prominent and most wealthy leaders in the Italian Socialist movement. Now a widow, she lives in Rome in a plush villa built on a courtyard much like this one in Warsaw where we now stood. Years ago, Mr. Blum told me, he took his son there to meet this remarkable woman. As they sat over lunch chatting in Yiddish, he said, she suddenly broke into tears when his son David joined into the Yiddish conversation.

"Why are you crying?" he asked her.

"It's your little boy," she replied. "I never thought I would ever again hear one so young speaking Yiddish. It's a miracle!"

Yes, a miracle. And a mystery. Along with a portion of his childhood, the old man had passed on to his son the language of his childhood. And in that language was contained the memory not only of one man's childhood but of an entire people. There can be no memory without the language. The word is a vessel of history that opens up a space where memory speaks. Who wouldn't weep at hearing Yiddish spoken by one so young? Hearing the Yiddish utterances of the child, perhaps the woman heard the voice of her own childhood.

After the scene in the courtyard I said my farewells and offered my deepest thanks to Mr. Blum and his son. They had given me a gift that few outsiders ever receive, not only by showing me the places where memories sleep but by showing me the importance of memory between a father and his child. They helped me to realize that memory is the most precious inheritance that we can pass on to our children. And they reminded me that the memory of a people rests on the memory that a single father may offer to a single child. Even dark memories can be transformed into light when they are thus transmitted. And Mr. Blum was kind enough to transmit his memories not only to his son but to me as well. I even learned a little Yiddish during the hours I spent with them.

One more treasure had been placed in my care. One more responsibility. God, give me the strength, the courage, and the character, to live up to it!

Back in the Novotel Hotel, I discovered that my black *kipah*, the one I had worn on the grounds of Treblinka, Majdanek, and Auschwitz-Birkenau had mysteriously disappeared. Just as the clock I had brought with me on this trip disappeared on my first day in Poland. Perhaps the message in this disappearance was that the head covering worn under a sky transformed into a cemetery should be left there. And that a timepiece brought to a land where time had been cast asunder is either useless or out of place or both.

I miss my family terribly: Gerri, Miriam, little Rachel. I constantly pray that they are well, but I cannot help worrying about them. When I arrive in Jerusalem, God willing, I shall call them. When, pray God, I hear Gerri tell me, "We're all fine," my heart will rejoice. It could use some rejoicing right now. Poland has been an overwhelming but a necessary strain. I feel that I have aged years, decades, centuries, as though I have taken on the age of the Chosen themselves, from the time of Our Father Abraham to this very day that commemorates the giving of the Torah at Sinai. I look into the mirror and notice that I have turned much more gray over the last few days.

Again my father's words come to my aid: Don't panic. Be not afraid. And with his words I hear the words of the Fathers: *Shma Yisrael, Adonai Elohenu, Adonai echad*—Hear, O Israel, the Lord is our God, the Lord is One. I have collided with a great mystery, its thread running from Treblinka to Majdanek, from Auschwitz to the Warsaw Synagogue. And from here I shall follow the blood-red thread all the way to Jerusalem.

But then there is this oppressive silence that yawns all around me, and in the silence the shriek....I swear this place is haunted!

Don't panic, my son.

I love you.

7 SIVAN 5751

Warsaw, 20 May 1991

ONCE AGAIN I AM UP at dawn to welcome the morning
light with my morning prayers. My flight for Tel-Aviv
leaves in a few hours. I have been to Israel twice before,
and on both occasions I looked forward to seeing it. But I
have never longed for the sight of the Judean Hills so
much as I do now. You don't go to Jerusalem, Elie Wiesel
once said, you return to it. *Teshuvah* is the word. It means
not only "return" but "response" and "redemption" as well.
For a Jew, a journey to Israel is an act of response, and
only through such an act of response and responsibility
can a Jew seek his redemption.

Today I go to a place where I seek a sense of belonging,
in an act of response and with the hope for redemption.
This thought takes on new meaning for me now, because
today I am going to Jerusalem—by way of Treblinka, Majdanek, Auschwitz, and the Warsaw Synagogue—for the
first time as a Jew. And I feel that, as a Jew, there is no
other route by which I may find a path to Israel. Perhaps,
ever since the Churban, all Jews may return to Jerusalem
only by way of Auschwitz, in one form or another. For the

souls of the dead accompany us every step of the way to the Holy Land.

One of the great Rabbis of our time, Rabbi Adin Steinsaltz, recently wished upon me the strength to bear the weight of the responsibility that comes with becoming a Jew. Upon hearing of my conversion he welcomed me to the fold, but with his welcome came a warning. Now I begin to understand a bit more of what that warning was about. To be a Jew is to be a light unto the nations in the midst of the Night that has fallen over the world. It means struggling to be in the right place at the right time, where the word joins with its meaning, in the cycles of darkness and light that go into life.

Has this trip made me a little bit more of a Jew? I do not know. It is not for me to say. But perhaps it has taken me to a deeper level in the eternal process of becoming a Jew. It has certainly taken me to a deeper level of accountability.

An elderly man who is from this country of Poland was among those who sat on the Bet Din for my conversion. In his Yiddish accent he cautioned me that in taking on a new name, I was taking on the memory of the Six Million. Jewish names are ridden with memory. Therefore they are overflowing with responsibility.

"Do you understand this?" he asked.

"Of course," I answered, and at the time I thought I was speaking the truth. But, of course, I had not the vaguest notion of what he was saying. Now, perhaps, I have at least a vague notion of what Mr. Slutzky was trying to tell me. How might I have answered him if I had known then what I think I know now?

I cannot wait to get out of Poland. The Poles have generally been kind to me, but that is not the point. It is the air and the earth that I find so oppressive here, the ghosts and the silence. Rather than say I am eager to leave Poland, it might be better to declare that I long to go to Israel and from Israel to my home, to my family. If my journey to Israel has taken me through Poland, my journey home will take me through Israel.

Indeed, I feel that, after what I have seen, the only way I can get back home is to pass through the Promised Land. I have much to do there in Erets Yisrael: my mission to the Wall, a return to Yad Vashem to know the place for the first time, my work on Russian-Israeli authors and Holocaust memoirs, people to visit, presence to establish, witness to bear. It is far more than I can do in the few days that I shall be there. But a man must always attempt more than he can do, if he is to become more as a man.

It rained all day yesterday. Poland has been overcast the entire week. Indeed, for the last fifty years a huge cloud has been hanging over this land. But this morning the sun is shining in a clear, blue sky. It is a good sign.

In the airport: I am sitting next to an Arab. It doesn't seem so difficult to sit quietly next to an Arab. When I arrived here a week ago I did not notice how small the International Terminal is. There are only three or four employees checking in travelers bound for destinations abroad. As I wait to show my passport, I cannot help thinking of the Wandering Jew. Do I fall into that category? I don't know. I am a traveling Jew, but that is not the same thing. Wandering is a condition of homelessness. The Jew is in a state of perpetual motion, yes. But the movement of wandering, the movement of exile, is a movement *from* the spot, while the movement of dwelling and becoming, which is the opposite of wandering, is a movement *at* the spot.

Perhaps Jerusalem is a place where the Wandering Jew may become the Dwelling Jew, if only the Jews of Jerusalem might learn to sit quietly next to an Arab. After all, perhaps above all, Judaism is the religion of dwelling, for dwelling happens precisely when the relation to one's family and neighbor is an expression of the relation to God. It happens where the path to oneself and to God leads through the other human being. It happens where love happens.

As the installation constructed to destroy God by destroying His Chosen, Auschwitz is the paradigm for the extreme opposite of a dwelling place. Instead of a Temple designed to emanate light, a crematorium built to swallow up light. Instead of the Temple Mount, a mound of ashes. Instead of an altar, a dissection table. Instead of the chamber of the Holy of Holies, the underground gas chamber. Instead of houses, blocks that served as warehouses where the raw material for the death factory was stored until the machine was ready for more fuel. Instead of ovens that bake bread for people to consume, ovens that consume people.

A woman standing near me is wearing a coat whose fabric reminds me of the fabric made of human hair that I saw at Auschwitz. A shudder runs through me. I am sure that her coat cannot be made of that ghastly material, but the image will not let go of me.

I have just moved into the third waiting area for the flight to Tel-Aviv. Among the people who fill the room are about two dozen Russian Jews and another couple of dozen Israelis. I hear Hebrew spoken here and there, as well as a bit of Russian, but most of the passengers are speaking Polish. Security seems to be very lax, especially for a flight to Israel.

Not far from me there is a man with no legs sitting in a wheelchair. He is smiling. Is he making *aliyah*?* There are several, more than several, old and infirm men and women on this flight. I wonder how many of them are going to Israel in order to die. They remind me of Rabbi Saul Liebermann, one of Elie Wiesel's teachers. On the day after he and Elie had finished their study of the Book of Ecclesiastes the Rabbi called his student to his office to

---

*Literally meaning "going up," this term signifies a Jew's taking up residence in Israel.

say good-bye.

"When I saw his clean desk," said Elie, "I knew that I would never see him again."

The Rabbi died in flight on his way to Jerusalem. The man rose to the heavens in an effort to make his way to the Land of the Fathers and never came down.

Right now the one thing I most look forward to is the sound of my wife's beautiful voice telling me that she and the girls are well. Dear God, please let it be so.

Time to board the flight.

⚱

Jerusalem, 20 May 1991

About an hour ago I checked into my room at Beit Belgia on the Givat Ram campus of Hebrew University. Just a few minutes ago I spoke to Gerri. She and my little girls and everyone else at home are well, thanks to the infinite goodness of the Holy One, blessed be He. My wife never sounded so good to me, and I don't think I have ever loved her so deeply.

Israel looks wonderful, feels wonderful, holy and whole, almost like...home. I broke down in tears of gratitude after hearing my wife. Even now there are tears in my eyes. I am all but ashamed at the blessedness of being here and hearing her voice. It is far more than I had longed for, far more than I had anticipated. Certainly more than I could ever hope to merit. I did not realize how abysmal was the pit of Poland until I came out of it. I am overcome by the *light* that floods this holy place. It is the light that was called forth upon the first utterance of Creation, the Light of God calling forth Himself, the Light that preceded the lights of the firmament, without which there can be no light, no firmament, no world, no life.

As soon as I entered the Ben Gurion Airport I noticed

the signs in Russian that were posted everywhere. The immigration of Russian Jews to Israel is overwhelming, a thousand or more each week, a number comparable to the influx of nearly a hundred thousand per week in the United States. The hospitality with which the Israelis welcome them is yet another indication of the resolve of this land and its people to provide a home to those Jews who are homeless.

Gerri's friend Liat, who has become my friend too, was kind enough to come from Jerusalem to meet me. She and Gerri met over twenty years ago, when they were attending Hebrew University together. I told her that she didn't have to make that long drive, but I was glad that she did. Liat is a good woman and a good Jew, one who exemplifies the Jewish characteristics of modesty, generosity, and lovingkindness. And in her these characteristics are all the more genuine because she is unaware of possessing them. Seeing her added a great deal to my feeling of having arrived in a land where I belong.

But as I listened to Liat's account of the days of the Gulf War, I was reminded that this is not yet *Gan Eden.** I almost wish that I had been here during that time. Something inside of me tells me that I should have been here. She described the relief that the people felt when the War finally started and then the fear that followed, the waiting for the sirens night after sleepless night, the waiting to see who would be hit next—Tel-Aviv, Haifa, Jerusalem? Would that madman use gas this time?

Fifty years ago the enemy herded the Jews into the gas chambers; next time they will bring the gas chambers to the Jews.

Jerusalem, of course, was spared. Liat told me that she took out her gas mask only a few times. I tried to picture that grotesque object covering her lovely face. I thought of

---

*Hebrew for "Garden of Eden," or paradise.

all the parents who had to place their babies in their cribs under protective coverings, and I recalled the Palestinian declarations that Saddam Hussein represented the highest values of the Arab world. What could the millions of good people among the Arabs have thought? What is a good man living in Iraq to do? Or has Saddam killed all their good men?

And then through my mind ran one of the most unforgettable images of the war, the image of Isaac Stern passionately playing his violin to an audience of people wearing gas masks. It is truly an image of Israel itself, in its affirmation of the dearness and the depth of life when life is most threatened. The courage and the faith of these people—a faith exemplified at times despite themselves—is staggering. I have never felt so humble about being a Jew, about struggling to become more and more of a Jew, despite all my failures. I have never felt so elated and yet so daunted about being an infinitesimal part of this People. I have never felt so much love for this People or so unworthy to count myself as one of them.

That love I feel even for the obnoxious, annoying, God-love-them Israelis on the flight from Warsaw. We sat on the ground for twenty minutes before taking off because a single seat had been assigned to two different people. Yes, there were other spaces available, but this one Israeli—a man decked out, jewelry and all, in the latest fashion—insisted on having *his* seat. After rearranging the positions of about eighteen people, he finally got his wish.

Then, once we were in the air, he and the other two dozen Israelis were out of their places and pacing up and down the aisle. I don't think he spent fifteen minutes of the three-and-a-half-hour flight in the spot he insisted on having. And, as if that were not enough, when it came time to land he took another seat!

It all reminded me of a comment that Rabbi Steinsaltz made to me two years ago, when I told him I was studying for conversion: the hardest thing about becoming a Jew, he said, is the Jews. But when I see a Jew who is less than Jewish, it only reminds me of how far I fall short myself.

O, how I love my wife! Her beautiful voice keeps coming back to me. Liat told me about how she and Gerri used to laugh so much and so hard when they were young. It was good to hear, and I was thankful that Gerri was able to enjoy such a friendship. I was happy for her, for Liat, and for the time when they laughed. Not all the young are so blessed with youth. I guess, to a large extent, youth is made of laughter. I only wish I had known her in those days when she laughed the laugh of youth. I wish I could have laughed with her then. But I am blessed far beyond merit or measure for knowing her now as my wife and as a mother to my two little girls. And suddenly it hits me: I am happy. Is it possible? Is it permissible, after where I have been and what I have seen?

I still have in my pocket, in my soul, a piece of the wall of the gas chamber in Auschwitz. Auschwitz, Birkenau, Treblinka, Majdanek, Dachau—I bear on my person fragments of all those places that signify the fragmentation of humanity. It lends a certain seriousness to my happiness. I suppose I am happy and grateful *despite* and, yes, *because of* what I carry inside of me. Happiness, like humor, is always serious business.

Thinking back on the Russian Jews who were on the flight from Warsaw to Tel-Aviv, I wonder whether they were coming to Israel or escaping from Russia. How many of them were doctors, lawyers, professors, and musicians who will have a very difficult time finding work as doctors, lawyers, professors, and musicians in Israel? Already I have heard Russian spoken here in Beit Belgia.

One of the ostensible reasons for my coming here is to study the outcry of these people. As ever, the problem of dwelling returns to me, and I am stricken by the critical role of the word in the problem of dwelling. We not only speak a language—we live in it. It is the house of our being. But in the case of the Russian-Israelis we have a people who in their native land were at home with the tongue but were strangers in the land itself. Here, on the other hand, they are at home in the land but are strangers to the tongue. The Russian-Israeli poet Mikhail Gendelev is one who addresses this difficulty which perhaps only poetry can address.

The problem of dwelling is a problem of joining place and word, of uttering the right word in the right place at the right time. Only then can meaning find its way into the word and into life. And only where meaning joins with the word to make life meaningful can a human being create a place to dwell. Therefore it is far more than a geographical problem. It is an existential and a metaphysical problem.

At Auschwitz meaning was severed from the word just as the human being was torn from his place, just as the bricks from the village Birkenau were made into the death camp Birkenau. Auschwitz is the paradigm of the Nonplace because Auschwitz is the epitome of the Nonword, of the great and solemn Silence of Nonbeing, the mute spokesman of Nothingness. But here in Jerusalem every Jew has a place. It is the site of the Indwelling Presence that stands over against the Imposed Absence that Auschwitz signifies. Jerusalem, therefore, is precisely the opposite of Auschwitz.

Lech Walesa flew to Israel this morning on a private jet. According to the local newscast, he addressed the Knesset, asking the Jews for forgiveness for what transpired on Polish soil. Perhaps he realizes that Poland can have no future as long as that past hangs over it. But it will not go away. Even forgiveness cannot make it go away. A Jew may forgive another for what he himself has suffered, but he may not offer forgiveness for the sufferings of others. Even if the dead child should forgive his torturer, even if the child's mother should grant forgiveness for her own suffering, she can never forgive the monster for what was done to her child.

So how can Poland *not* live in the shadow of its past? And how can the Jews offer Mr. Walesa anything but a resolute silence in response to his request?

The news also reported several murders, with both Arabs and Israelis among the victims. In each instance the issue of "national motive" was raised. I don't understand this. How can nationality be a motive for murder? What do people serve, in the name of what do they act, when they kill individuals on the street for the sake of nationality? What does that make of one's nationality? No, I do not understand. It seems to me that a man who murders in the name of his nation betrays his nation.

Sometimes, Liat once told me, when she hears that a Jew has been killed, she almost wishes that the murderer might be another Jew, just so that more hatred will not arise among the Jews. For this hatred toward the other invariably destroys us from within.

Just now I was going through my things, and I found the *kipah* I wore at the concentration campsites. It disappeared for a time, but now that I have returned to Israel, it has returned to me.

Tomorrow the Wall.

8 SIVAN 5751

Jerusalem, 21 May 1991

YOU DON'T GO TO Jerusalem—you return to it. Yes. But I would add: you return *within* it. The Jews who live here undertake a continual movement of *teshuvah*, at times without realizing it, by helping others to return to the Land of the Fathers. Only when I open my home to the other does it become a home, where life may return to itself. The observance of Passover, for example, is an observance of the deliverance from exile and a return home; and an important part of that observance is opening the door to our home and inviting all who are hungry to join us at our table. Abraham also comes to mind: after he opened his home to the three strangers, the three angels, it was announced that Sarah would bear the child Isaac. The two events are bound together: life happens where life is allowed to enter.

When Liat told me yesterday about feeling that she must do something for her Russian neighbors, I recognized a definitive tie between the People and the Land. In Poland the Chosen are linked to the land through the ashes that cover it. Here the link is not land to ashes but land to flesh and blood, a bond made of that lovingkindness which goes into the making of a Jew. Those who were born on this soil and who are thus made of it offer themselves to others who seek a home here. Thus offering themselves, they offer their land: land for peace.

Liat is herself a perfect example. She not only provided her new Russian neighbors with furniture and other goods, but she offered to teach them the language and to get them into the Ulpan, the language center where they may learn to speak Hebrew. After that, if they wished, she would help them to learn English. I was particularly struck by this. Offering them this gift of the word, she was offering up a part of her soul—not just part of her time but part of her lifetime.

Once again I could see still more evidence that being at home in the land lies in being at home in the word. But being at home in the word entails much more than learning a language. It entails making your soul, your life, into a place where word and meaning are wed. It requires a capacity for the betrothal to the Holy One that we affirm each day when we wind the *tefillin* around the middle finger. It demands a capacity for response, for modesty, generosity, and lovingkindness—*to* the other person and *for* the other person. *Home* lies within the other human being, or rather in that space between an I and a Thou where the Eternal Thou is made manifest.

Liat told me that some kibbutzniks wanted to host a large number of the Russian immigrants for a Passover Seder, but the Orthodox rabbis would not allow it. Although my inclinations are toward the Orthodox, I wonder about the wisdom of this decision. The rabbis, of course, based their decision on a strict observance of the letter of the Law. But according to aggadic tradition, the evil of Sodom did not lie in the wild and indiscriminate behavior of its inhabitants; rather the city fell into evil as a result of legislation that combined malice with an overzealousness for the letter of the law. I think it is better to have some kind of a Seder, even if it is not according to the letter of Orthodoxy, than to have no Seder. The spirit needs the letter, yes, just as the soul needs the body. But the path to the letter can lead through the spirit, particularly when the spirit is manifested as joy.

Most of the Russian Jews, even the youngest among them, can remember the time when it was unlawful in the Soviet Union to study Hebrew or anything else Jewish. Subsequently, most of them know very little about their heritage. They have never read a Bible, much less participated in a Passover Seder. The Seder is, among other things, about the deliverance from just this sort of oppression. Who, then, might know more about rejoicing in their deliverance from such slavery, the slavery of not being allowed to be who you are, than these Russian Jews?

It seems to me that in their rejoicing alone they might have taught their hosts something about being Jewish. As a Hasidic Master once told his followers, "your song and dance count for more than my sermons." After what I have seen in Poland, this isolation of Jew from Jew is more painful to me than ever. The Jew should be the symbol of proximity between human beings, not a sign of distance and separation. The word *seder* means "order," and for a Jew order comes in the loving relation to another Jew.   Rejoicing together can engender that relation, and the ability to rejoice has never been so urgently needed.

When I spoke to Gerri on the phone yesterday, she told me that Miriam will be at home this coming Shabbat and that Rachel was spending a lot of time playing with her grandfather, Gerri's dad. Although they are seventy years apart, the closeness between Rachel and her "Paka," as she calls him, is what home and family are all about. I shall take my family with me when I go to the *Kotel*, the Western Wall, this morning. And I shall take six million others....

On the way to the Wall: I took a bus from the Givat Ram campus to the Central Bus Station. From there I had to pass through an underground tunnel to get to the stop for the bus that goes to the Old City. Here and there the walls were defaced with graffiti, but it included none of the foul words that one often sees in other cities. *Love* was the four-letter word that appeared most frequently. And in the tunnel, in the darkness of the underground, sat an old beggar, hand out and eyes cast down. I remembered the money that Gerri gave to me when I left home.

"This is for the first beggar you see in Jerusalem," she said.

It is a Jewish custom to entrust a traveler with something for a beggar. That way his journey becomes a mission to perform a *mitzvah*, and so God goes with him.

I reached into my pocket, and, from among the three stones that I carried there, I withdrew my wife's offering for the old man sitting in the tunnel. I touched his hand, and for an instant I reached into his darkness, and his darkness reached into me. I remembered the words of a Hasidic Master: I am afraid of nothing, but the sight of a beggar sends shudders through me. Is it you, Eliyahu? After all, we are told that one of your favorite disguises for walking the earth is that of a beggar.

I realized that this destitute old man was among the gatekeepers along the road to the *Kotel*. And the toll for passing through his gate was not the coins I placed in his hand but the demand that I look upon his face. There was no getting to the Wall except by way of that implication. He didn't say a word to me, but his silence is still ringing in my ears. Perhaps he could not speak. Handing him the silver coins, I wanted to thank him, but, more than that, I wanted to beg this beggar's forgiveness. For I had the distinct feeling that he was sitting there in my place. Were it not for the grace of *Hashem*....

The bus to the Western Wall passed through *Meah She'-*

arim, a neighborhood where Hasidim of various schools live. Its name means "One Hundred Gates," signifying the gates through which God enters the world and through which people may find their way to God. Through those gates they filed onto the bus, many of them bearing in their arms the religious texts that contain God's Word and convey His Presence. And yet, as we rode past their shops and their houses of study, I was again flooded with the insanely contrasting images of the death camps. I reached for the stones in my pocket and took them into my hand. Warm with life, they reminded me of how I got here and of where I was going.

An old man sitting in front of me was studying one of the tractates of the Talmud of the Order *Moed*, which deals with the Holy Days. It fits, I thought to myself. The Holy Days are those segments of time when the Eternal enters the hour, just as the Infinite, the *En Sof*, has entered this place, this neighborhood, this very bus. I have never seen a greater fulfillment of the idea of *community*, of the gathering of a people about a single, transcendent center that joins each to the other, each to all, apparent in their every gesture. A part of me wanted to get off the bus and linger there in that neighborhood. But I had business at the Wall.

Across the aisle from another Hasid sat an Israeli soldier. He had an automatic weapon slung over his shoulder. Looking at this striking pair, I thought of the injunction *zachor v'shamor*, remember and observe, remember and watch over, remember and protect. How commonplace is the extraordinary, the miraculous, in this remarkable land! If the Hasid himself were not enough to bear witness to the Indwelling Presence that abides here, this overwhelming contrast would drive the point home. Each of them sat calmly, quietly, while I was about to swoon, mostly with gratitude to both of them. The image of myself taking up residence here with my wife and my children came all too naturally. It felt so right.

At the gate to the *Kotel* I encountered more beggars, more gatekeepers who announced the depth of my debt. Among them were a Hasid and two or three women. All of them looked as though they bore a weariness as ancient as the Wall itself. I gave them money and then proceeded past the soldiers and toward the Wall. Their cries of "*Adon, Adon! Todah raba!*"—"Sir, Sir! Thank you very much!"—followed after me like a benediction that I did not deserve. Indeed, how can a man deserve anything that a beggar offers him, even if it is just a word of thanks?

Suddenly my steps slowed down. I mustn't rush this, I told myself. I mustn't hurry over this ground where the history of the world, where God's presence in history, is continually decided. My legs begin to shake at the thought of what lies beneath my feet. Indeed, I find it impossible to move any faster, for the piece of that dreadful wall that I carry in my pocket now seems as heavy as the Wall itself. Will I be able to lift it? Coming from Treblinka, Majdanek, and Auschwitz-Birkenau to this Holy Site, I have traveled from one end of the universe to the other, from absolute Absence to absolute Presence, from total darkness to blinding light. Is that what our lives are about? To be haunted by absence and blinded by presence?

With an utterance of the appropriate blessing, I wash my trembling hands and thus "raise them up," as the blessing goes. Then, taking the *talit* and *tefillin* from my bag, I begin my approach to the Wall. From within it and from beyond it holiness radiates like a field of gravity drawing me toward its center.

As I near the ancient stones, I can see the thousands of slips of paper inserted into the cracks, their prayers sent through this portal to the ears of *HaShem.* Around me there are some two dozen Jews lost—or rather found—in prayer. Swaying to and fro, they peer into their prayer books through thick eyeglasses, their sight given over to the texts of the Holy Word, so that they might truly see.

Several other witnesses to the faith are sitting off to the side of the Wall discussing Torah and Talmud. I marvel at the realization that they spend whole days here, day after day, in the shadow of the invisible Temple.

Now standing at the Wall, I reach out to touch its massive stones, and another stone, the one I have brought here, speaks to me in a thin voice of silence, a *kol demamah dakah*: "The hour is at hand! Into the Wall! From that wall to this, from death to life! Each wall will be transformed!"

As though moving in slow motion, I unfold my *talit* and wrap myself in the Light of the Holy One. More slowly still I unravel my *tefillin* to lay the sign upon my arm and place the word between my eyes. The songs of prayer all around me, the songs of the Hasidim and others among the pious, fill my ears.

And through the songs I can hear the voice urging me on: "Into the Wall! Into the Wall!"

Despite my trembling, I manage to don my *talit*, lay my *tefillin*, and open my *siddur*.

Despite my tears, I manage to read the prayers, the *Adon Olam*, the *Shma*, the *Shmoneh Esrei*, and others. Taking care over every syllable, I search the recesses of my soul for the *kavanah* and the *hitlahavut*, the intensity and the passion, that might impart to each word its meaning and its truth. Although I am standing at the bottom of the towering Wall, I have the sensation of soaring above it. "Open my lips, O Lord, that I may sing Your praise!" We think we pray to the Holy One, blessed be He, but that is not precisely the case, for the prayer itself is divine. The prayer itself has wings.

Finally, I turn to the back of the prayerbook, to the *Kaddish* and other prayers for the dead. But this time I have the distinct feeling that these are the prayers *of* the dead. I can almost hear the voices curled up in the fragment from the other wall praying with me, until, coming to the end of the prayers, I tenderly take it in hand, press it to my lips, and place it in the Wall among the slips of paper with their inscriptions and supplications.

This tiny piece of concrete is more than a link that would make darkness into light. Brought from Auschwitz to Jerusalem, it comes from the time of the world's destruction to a timelessness that precedes the Creation. It is itself a prayer of stony silence, a prayer therefore of deafening outcry once swallowed up in the night, now turned over to the Temple Light. This bit of stone has the prayers of six million invisibly and inaudibly inscribed upon it, and now those prayers are joined with the others that inhabit the Wall, a piece of the Eternal returned to Himself.

Having accomplished this mission, I turned, reluctantly, to leave. An overwhelming part of me wanted to dwell there until the end of my days. But a pilgrim is not meant to stay. He has duties that lie elsewhere. And I realized that I might continue to dwell on this site only by taking it home with me to my family.

As I exited through the gate, I was once again assailed by beggars. Among them was a Hasid who asked me my name and laid his hands on my head to recite a blessing over me, in return for what I had given him. Then he tied a red thread around my wrist, binding me to all those for whom I gave my *tsedakah*, connecting me, in my responsibility, to all who are in need, to the widow, the orphan, and the stranger who incessantly call my name.

"Why the red thread?" I wondered. Then it occurred to me that perhaps it is a custom that goes back to the story of Rahab and the spies whom she helped, as the Israelites were preparing to enter the Promised Land. When Joshua sent the two men into the Land to obtain information, Rahab gave them refuge in her home. As they left, they told her to tie a red thread around her window lattice, so that when the Israelites came to claim the city, they would see the thread as a sign of one who had offered help to God's Chosen. According to tradition, Rahab became a proselyte.

I left them behind me, but the beggars continued to call after me. I can still hear their plaintive call.

In the course of going to and from the Western Wall I circled the Old City, the center of the universe. The north and northeast sides of the wall that surrounds the City were lined with Arab shops, Arab men and women and children. They looked so sad to me, so…homeless. Once again I could not help wondering whether we can truly build a home and thus create a place to dwell when there are so many homeless human beings in our midst. The faces of the Arab children, with their beseeching eyes, disturbed me most of all. Would it ever be possible for them to grow up to be more than second-class citizens of this Jewish state? And how can it be a *Jewish* state if it continues to have second-class citizens?

Looking upon them, I ached with a longing for peace, as these people, Jews and Arabs alike, must ache. Surely that ache alone might be a tie that binds Arab and Jew together. Surely that ache alone, as it ages the children of both, might be a reason to love one another, to save the children, and to erase every trace of anything that would go into the making of such places as Auschwitz and Majdanek. For as long as there is hatred and the homelessness that it breeds, there will be paths that ultimately lead to the death camp.

Yesterday Liat told me that the children of the survivors in Israel are experiencing exactly the same fears, nightmares, and neuroses as their parents. And, she added, they go through this suffering whether their parents have spoken to them of the Event or not. It seems that the survivors radiate their memory, silently and ineluctably. It isn't just in their mind—it's in every cell of their flesh and blood, in the very stuff of which they and their children are made. You cannot be around them without being around the Event.

I too have been infected. Every Jew is infected. The world is infected. Mr. Slutzky warned me. The ashes filled with the memory were launched from the chimneys and cast upon the winds to settle over the face of the earth. With every breath we breathe we draw them into our lungs. They have become part of the grain from which we make our bread, and as we eat, we become heirs to the ashes. They infest the milk of mothers' breasts and thus become part of the bodies of us all from birth.

It sounds farfetched? Perhaps. But this inherited memory explains so much of the madness that plagues us. And yet the one thing that may redeem us from that madness is memory itself. As we are told in the Talmud, God heals through the same means by which He afflicts. And memory is both affliction and healing. We must remember, not to keep it from happening again, but to be afflicted and healed and thus to keep from going mad. Or to pursue madness to its very end. As oblivion is tied to exile, said the Baal Shem Tov, so is memory tied to redemption.

9 SIVAN 5751

Jerusalem, 22 May 1991

I SPOKE TO A FRIEND named Chaim Gouri on the phone last night. I met him two years ago, when I was here in Israel doing some work at the Hebrew University Library. It was he who introduced me to the Russian-Israeli poet Mikhail Gendelev. I hope Gouri can arrange something for me with Gendelev this trip. He said he would call me at around eight this morning to set a time when I might pay him a visit. His wife just came out of the hospital and is recovering from an operation, so he naturally wants to stay close by her.

Once more I am reminded of my wife and of how much I miss her. She too had an operation just a few months ago. More and more I realize that in some very deep ways the tale of this journey from Auschwitz to Jerusalem is a love story. It isn't just the absence that makes the heart grow. It is a greater understanding of what must be inscribed upon the heart and offered to the other. In the Talmud we are told that a man is not a man until he takes a wife. And in the Midrash there is an even stronger statement: a man is not a man without a woman, a woman is not a woman without a man, and both need God to be who they are. This is what we are taught in the tale of the Creation: male and female created He them. (For a long time I have thought that the sum of life's truth and depth is contained in the first four chapters of Genesis; all the rest is commentary.)

Like the creation of a human life, the creation of a marriage requires three. As the place where life comes into being, the relation between husband and wife is the root and branch of the relation to the Holy One and therefore to all that is holy. When the sacredness of marriage is lost, so is all else that is sacred. The whole of Creation nestles in the space between husband and wife, and this has staggering implications. For one thing, it means that the nature of the marital relation may hide the darkness that leads to Auschwitz, or it may harbor the light that leads to Jerusalem. Yes, it all begins there. It all begins with me. Whatever the event, said the Kotzker Rebbe, *you* are its origin. You are the one in responsibility. And the seeds of all events are planted in the relation between husband and wife. If God is not revealed in that relation, then He is not revealed anywhere. That is why it is said that Israel gathered at Sinai as a bride come to meet her groom. And, in times of evil, that is why the prophets denounced the Chosen as a harlot.

Today I must go to Yad Vashem on the Mount of Remembrance. Yesterday I was at the Temple Mount, which, according to tradition, is Mount Moriah, the site of the Binding of Isaac. Today I go to the Mount of Remembrance. The two are linked, and they demand that I become a bridge between them. In fact, they form the borders of Jerusalem and therefore the horizons of the earth. One tells us what to remember; the other tells us why. On Mount Moriah Abraham raised an altar. On the Mount of Remembrance the angel who stayed his hand raised a memory and a name: Yad Vashem.

The phrase "Mount of Remembrance" has a nice nuance. It reminds us that memory is our one means of overcoming the force of gravity that weighs on us, the one path that may lead us out of exile. Memory is an ascent, a rising up, like the movement of *aliyah*. *Aliyah*, the movement of return, is a movement of memory, and memory is a movement of *aliyah*, a response, a *teshuvah*. How, then, can I come to Israel without going to the Mount of Remembrance? I have not arrived here until I have been there.

On the way to the Mount: Once again I must change buses at the Central Bus Station. Once again I encounter a beggar. This time it is a middle-aged woman dressed in rags. She too was once a little girl, fresh and full of life, with a mother who loved her. Perhaps she grew up to become a mother herself. Where is her mother now, where her children?

Sprawled out on the sidewalk, the woman is bent over a prayer book lying on the pavement, her face just inches from the ground. It is as if she were about to move into the earth itself. Once again I pay the toll to the gatekeeper and silently beg the beggar's forgiveness. Her eyes are still riveted to the prayers. Is it possible that among them there will be a prayer for my soul? I have the feeling that if this might be so, then perhaps I may somehow find redemption after all. Her image follows me into the bus for the Mount of Remembrance.

Twenty minutes later I step off the bus and head up the forested hill toward Yad Vashem. The trees create a calm that is not exactly a calm. Once on the grounds of the place of remembrance, I go first to the Children's Memorial. At its entrance there are several pillars of stone, each one broken like a branch torn from a petrified tree. The structure of the Memorial is framed in stone and built into a hill, under the ground, like a tomb.

The first thing to hit you when you go in are the portraits of a few of the million and a half little ones who perished in the flames. Their eyes are flooded with sadness and fear. They drain every human being who comes before them of every feeble excuse and demand to know: "Where are you?" I force myself to look into those eyes, and I cannot control the tears that flow from my own eyes. I long to take them into my arms, but they are no more. Why, dear God? *Why?* And in the midst of the question their images echo the impotence of asking.

My knees grow weak under the weight of their eyes, and I realize that the handrail running through this tomb is not just to guide you through the darkness. Indeed, nothing can point the way through this darkness filled with a million and a half points of light, like distant stars from another universe. No, the handrail is there for you to hold on to as you pass from this world and into their world, lest you swoon and fall.

I can hear the rumbling that I heard rolling under the stones of Treblinka and over the ashes of Majdanek, the rumbling that is neither sound nor the absence of sound, neither being nor nothingness. It vibrates along the blackened passageway, and through the rumbling, one by one, resound the names and the ages of little boys and little girls who were consumed by another darkness. Yakov, six years old; Shimon, four years old; Sarah, seven years old. And on and on and on and on, a memory and a name, *yad vashem*, for each receding beam of light created here by the interplay of candles and mirrors that line the floor, walls, and ceiling. And through each name there is One who calls my name, One who asks me whether I am indeed Avraham David ben Avraham.

You don't walk through the Children's Memorial—you fall through it, clinging to the handrail, staggering with every step, losing every bearing. You can't see because you can't stop the tears. Every utterance of every name drains from you another drop of your soul, a tear for every name, a sob for every candle, until you wonder whether the cup of tears on high will ever be filled, whether the Messiah will ever come. Did he die after all with these children? Clutching the rail, I struggle onward, and still the chanting of the names goes on and on and on and on. Will it never end? What is this place? Why is it here? How can the earth bear it? When will the heavens break?

"It is as though the killers knew precisely what the children meant to us," Elie Wiesel once said. "According to our tradition, the world subsists thanks to them." But these children were crushed under the weight of an indifferent world.

In the Midrash it is written that when the First Temple fell and the priests were sent into exile, the *Shechinah*, God's Indwelling Presence, nonetheless remained. Then the Levites were compelled to leave, but still the *Shechinah* continued to dwell in the Holy Land. But when the children were taken away, the *Shechinah* herself was forced into exile. And how, then, will the world subsist?

The darkness in the Children's Memorial and its myriad of tiny flames reveal the lie and the illusion that the world goes on. Ever since the extinguishing, the murder, of these lights, the world has turned into an illusion, a wasteland of homelessness. Home is where the child dwells, and there is no dwelling for any man who does not create a place of dwelling for the child. It seems that now the only place where the child dwells is the nonplace framed by the Children's Memorial, a place of memory, a place of the remembrance of what it is too late to protect.

Emerging from the Children's Memorial, I am blinded by the daylight that penetrates through the clouds overhead. I sit down and struggle to jot down these notes. It is starting to rain. The sky itself cannot restrain its tears. They fall over this very page.

After regaining a shameful semblance of composure, I move on to the Holocaust Memorial, the one with a flame rising up from the floor, its column of smoke passing through an opening in the ceiling, like an eternal offering placed on the altar of memory. The guardian at the door offers me a cardboard *kipah* but then notices that I am wearing one. Walking around the edge of the railing, I trace the edges of an abyss, and on its surface float the names of places where other flames soared into the heavens. Among them are names now infamous: Auschwitz, Treblinka, Belzec, Majdanek, Chelmno, Bergen-Belsen, Dachau, Buchenwald, Mauthausen. And then there are names that are perhaps not so widely known but are just as horrid: Klooga, Westerbork, Drancy, Stutthof, Ponary.

Casting its light over these names, the flame on the floor is itself bathed in the light that comes through the opening in the roof and from beyond that opening. Yet this large room is dim, dim despite the light, as dim as memory. Here light does battle with darkness, as it reaches for light, touches light, cuts into the eyes, bores into the soul. The struggle between light and darkness is unfair, says Wiesel. Light always wins. But the darkness is not defeated. It goes into hiding. Where does it hide? Inside the light.

The Children's Memorial is made of darkness punctuated with points of light. This one is made of light punctuated with points of darkness. And both are made of stone and silence, the signs of the lifelessness that swallowed up the life of the world. In each place there are names that summon by name every human being who enters, names of life and names of death, names that snatch away a piece of your own name, so that no one leaves here whole.

Names: *Shemot*. It is the Hebrew title of the Book of Exodus. There is no exodus, no return from exile without the invocation of names, without the embrace of the Name. A remark made by Miguel de Unamuno comes to mind: "Tell me thy name!" means the same as "Save my soul!" For in the Name lies my memory, as well as a memory that is not my own. Made of memorials, Yad Vashem is made of names, as its own name suggests. It is built from the names of the children uttered in the Children's Memorial and from the names that reside in the Hall of Names. Together they form one long, formless Name that cannot be named or contained in the seventy letters of the Ineffable Name.

It is said that the Name of the Holy One consists of all the words of the Torah put together. But now I am not so sure. I think that perhaps His name may consist of all these names, for every name in the Torah was borne by those who died in the flames of the death camps. At Auschwitz people were robbed of their names and tattooed with numbers, a process calculated to rob them and the rest of the world of their memory. Here those names are resurrected, despite the efforts of some to forget and thus to murder the dead yet again. Standing here, I feel as though I have been swept over by a huge tidal wave of names, my own name lost in its watery depths.

Between the Memorial and the museum there is a sculpture of an emaciated, faceless man wrapped in *talit* and *tefillin,* his bony hands clutching his head. It is titled "The Silent Scream." Is that what our prayers have been made into? Perhaps in this world that is the only means we have left of praying.

I walk past another sculpture on my way into the Museum. It is a statue of Job in the midst of outcry, a sentry who silently stands watch over this entrance to the Kingdom of Memory. Looking over my left shoulder, I wonder for an instant whether he will rise from his pedestal and follow me.

In the museum I make my way through the artwork, the photographs, the historical accounts, all of which I have looked at before but which I have yet to see. For a long time I stand and stare at the famous picture of Elie in the barracks of Buchenwald at the time of his liberation.

This is the child whose childhood was destroyed, who witnessed the hanging of God on the gallows of Buna, who would tell his story in a book called *Night*, and who would become one of the scribes of Israel. Above him is Mr. Mermelstein, the man who brought suit against the revisionists in Los Angeles and won. And the others? Where are they now? Where in their memory is this scene of biblical intensity locked away?

Then there was an even more startling photo, equally famous. Yehiel De-Nur, the author known as Ka-tzetnik, used to keep a copy of it posted over his writing desk. It is a portrait of a barefoot Jew wrapped in his *talit*, in his *tefillin*, and in his prayers. Next to him is a row of bodies, Jews just shot by the Nazi soldiers who stand behind him grinning, laughing, mocking him for his devotion to God. Already this man has crossed over to the other shore, to the place where the murderers are about to send him. On his face the look of concentration, of wholeness and holiness, is staggering.

Think of it! Standing on the brink of the void, he nonetheless gathers himself into his prayers, so great is this man's faith! Looking upon this image of righteousness, I am implicated in my weakness and taught how to pray, even though the serpent may wrap itself about my feet.

But on this day my most severe collision in the museum was with a small glass display case. It contained the miniature shoe that once covered the right foot of a child as he took the last steps of his short life. The shoes piled chest-deep in Majdanek and Auschwitz once again coil around my heart. I am drowning in a sea of shoes made of a single tiny shoe left in a room adjacent to a gas chamber, fetched from that pit and brought here to rest on this hilltop known as the Mount of Remembrance. How can a man ever fill *those* shoes? And if he does not, how can he be a man?

The darkened room is flooded with a maelstrom of ghosts and eyes that ooze infinite urgency, with faces ravaged by the evil and the indifference of the faceless. Everywhere there are names, names born by human beings of whom all that is left is a name, names that speak far more than the texts that frame the exhibits. In a way, the exhibits veil what they are intended to reveal. They are too ordered to convey the chaos and the collapse of order, too neatly organized to communicate the overturning of values, of all frontiers, of all possibility. Something in me wants to smash them and send them across the floor and cry out to the people around me, "This is it! Can't you see?"

I am dizzy, exhausted, drained, scattered. How much more of this can I stand? I want to leave it all, but it won't leave me. Choosing has nothing to do with it. I am chosen before I choose, summoned before I decide. Six million names cover my name like a shroud, and forevermore I must identify myself by the name of the other, by my capacity to answer to and for these names. I am terrified. The voices of the Polish peasants who called me by the name of "Yisraeli" echo in my ears, and again I am overcome with the shame of my cowardice. Avraham David ben Avraham, where are you?

I am poured out like water. My heart melts in the midst of my bowels. *Selah.*

I go outside, making an effort not to run. It is pouring down rain. Blood from the sky. For each drop a name. The sky cannot contain it. I am soaked to the bone...

When I changed buses at the Central Bus Station to return to Givat Ram the same beggar was there, still bent over her prayer book. It struck me that if you wanted to behold the eternity of the Eternal One, you would have to look no further than this beggar. I had spent several hours at Yad Vashem, but it seemed that in all that time she had not moved. And yet she looked different somehow. Or was

I the one who was different?

I arrived at the campus with enough time to go to the library for a short while. I did not find very much on Russian-Israeli authors. I guess the topic is still too new. Perhaps when I go through the issues of *Dvadtsat' dva* (a Russian literary journal whose title means "Twenty-Two") something will turn up. I did find a book titled *Holocaust Memoirs* that I should examine tomorrow. Right now I am about to leave for Gouri's apartment. Perhaps he can help me with the names of some of the Russian-Israeli writers. But I want to ask him about his coverage of the Eichmann trial and his writing of *The Man in the Glass Cage*, as well as about the making of his film *The Eighty-First Blow*.

More when I get back...

I have just returned from my talk with Gouri. Unfortunately, I was unable to tape our conversation. It just didn't seem to be appropriate. Some of Mrs. Gouri's relatives were there visiting her. I was thankful to see that she is recovering nicely from her surgery. She is a good woman. And Gouri is an amazing man.

Under the circumstances, I did not get to speak with him about all the things that I had wanted to discuss, but we did go over some urgent matters, and he wants to see me again tomorrow. He told me about his own visit to Majdanek ten years ago. His voice shook with emotion when he related how devastated he was when he encountered the inscription "In every handful of ashes I seek my brother."

"A dark cloud of Jewish souls hovers over Poland," he said to me.

I could see that a piece of his soul hovers there too.

Gouri has a profound love for the forgotten and an equally profound longing for a just world. Not long after the war, when he was a young man, he traveled from Israel in his capacity as a journalist to a refugee camp that housed a number of survivors. His novel *The Chocolate Deal* is set in those days right after the war. "Just as there are earthquakes," he wrote, "so are there timequakes." In the refugee camp he met with a realityquake. There he came across the harsh living conditions shared by survivors from all over Europe.

"This place is hell," he commented to a young woman.

"Hell?" she answered. "Gouri, you are a poet, and a poet must be more careful with his words. This isn't hell. Hell is something else."

On her arm, he told me, was the number tattooed at Auschwitz.

He was kind enough to show me two of his poems recently translated into English. One was about Ahab and Elijah, the king and his prophet, whom Gouri described as "the shadow of the king." It was a poem that explored the depths of accountability, of human authority and divine summons. As I read it, I was reminded of the Commandment that a king must write out the entire Torah, so that he may know that his word is neither the first nor the last word. And I was reminded of a time in Germany when the utterance of the Fuehrer was the equivalent of law. When that happens, when the king loses the prophet, Auschwitz happens.

Israel appears to be made of this tension between king and prophet, from the time of Samuel and Saul, Nathan and David, even until now, each needing the other to become who he is. It is true that there are no prophets among us (or are there?), but the influence of the Rabbinate upon the State is immense. In the tension between the two, in the polarity from which each determines his essence, lies responsibility. The prophet signifies for the king that he, the king, is chosen before he chooses, chosen by the Good before choosing between good and evil. And the king signifies for the prophet the charge placed in his, the prophet's, care; he signifies the prophet's answering to *HaShem* in his calling forth to the king.

Between the two truth rises up. Between the two Israel has arisen, despite a mountain of ashes that buried all the prophets and choked all the kings.

Gouri spoke to me, too, about the death some time ago of twenty Israeli children. They died, horribly, when their school bus collided with a train. He told me of a certain Orthodox rabbi who, apparently reading the thoughts of the Holy One, insisted that these little ones, these lambs of God, were killed because most Israelis fail to observe the Sabbath. Thus he offered his words of solace to the mothers and fathers of those children. Nothing happens by chance or accident, said the Rav.

True. But to declare the *why* of such an event is to eliminate the *why* and thus presume a knowledge of the mystery of the Creator and His Creation, of the very mystery that we are summoned to remember and observe each Shabbat. Such a declaration amounts to the heretical presumption of equating oneself with God. It is to assert that I, the Rav, know what God knows. If, as Rambam contends, what God knows is what God is, then the rabbi's judgment amounts to the declaration that he is God. And, as we all know, there is no greater blasphemy. In this case it is a blasphemy that adds death to death. The fear of God is the opposite of this fear that the so-called rabbi would engender, which is the fear of mishap, of chance and accident.

What would such a man say about the deaths of the million and a half children who perished in the *Shoah*? If their deaths have no meaning, Wiesel once wrote, it is an outrage. And if those deaths do have a meaning, it is an even greater outrage.

For some reason I am reminded of a story about Beruriah, the wife of the Talmudic Sage Rabbi Meir. At the close of one Shabbat she went to her husband and asked him a question.

"If someone has entrusted you with two precious gems," she wanted to know, "do you have to return them when he comes to claim them?"

"Of course," the Rabbi answered.

"Well," said his wife, "God has come in the night to claim his gems. Our two children are dead."

And what if He should come to claim six million? What if He should demand not only the precious gems but the ones to whom their light is entrusted? What then?

10 SIVAN 5751

Jerusalem, 23 May 1991

Last night sleep came later than usual, and with it, once again, came disturbing dreams. I suppose that, in a way, every pilgrimage into the soul entails a journey into dreams. My recollection of the dreams is disjointed, but I remember being somehow forced to paint a large sign, a billboard. It was supposed to be a portrait of Stalin. As I painted it, his cruel face began to move, as though coming to life, and beneath it, in cursive letters, blood-red, was written the caption "The reason why is. . . ." There seemed to be more after the word *is,* but I could not make it out. And I could not make the face speak.

As I write these lines, the rabbi whom Gouri told me about, the one who gave the reason for the deaths of the twenty school children, comes to mind. Twenty children: one for each of the twenty million victims of the Russian tyrant. Those children were the victims not only of the collision with the train—they were the rabbi's victims as well. He was feeding on them, like a vulture, to serve himself, not God, to advance his own power. Is that what the vision means?

Then the dream shifted, and suddenly I was riding in a car. Elie Wiesel was driving. He took me to a dark auditorium, much like the one I had seen at Yad Vashem, where college-age and teenage students were watching a film about the terrible atrocities committed at Auschwitz. He pointed out to me a young lady who was crying, and then another, and still another. He told me to take care of them, all of them, and to protect the dead. And then he left. I went over to one girl and tried to comfort her as best I could, as if she were one of my own children. I realized that this comfort and compassion were far more needful than any explanations of what they were seeing. Indeed, they understood some small part of it. Their tears told me so.

Soon the film ended, and another student, also a young woman, stood up laughing and shouted, "Auschwitz was good for those people! It was good for all people!"

And I realized what Elie had meant when he told me to take care of these youths and to protect the dead. I quickly walked up to this young lady and firmly demanded, "Why was it good for them? What makes murder good?"

But she was unable to answer. Like the face of Stalin, hers moved, but it did not speak.

At that point the auditorium was transformed into something like a gymnasium where athletic games are held, and seated in the stands were various gangs of teenagers. Organ music was dramatically playing in the background, and a woman was prompting a member of one gang to fire a weapon at another gang, with the musical accompaniment calculated to lend suspense to the scene. Was she the same as the one who had declared Auschwitz to be a good thing? I broke up the gathering and went over to the woman who had tried to get one youth to fire at another. I asked her why she was encouraging murder, making it into a perverted game. She merely laughed, and I felt a great evil emanating from her. She told me then that my boss, the president of my university, would be angry with me for dispersing the crowd. She said it would lower enrollment.

I think I see in these dreams something of what threatens life and the message that these threats are often made into something very attractive, like the Sirens who lure sailors seeking new horizons to their deaths. When you walk the grounds of Auschwitz-Birkenau, what you see all around you is one huge sign of all that threatens life. What remains invisible to the eye is the precious and fragile essence of the life that is threatened. This stark juxtaposition of the deadly and the dear has the power to warn and thus to preserve, if only we can overcome our fatal indifference, our pathological deafness, to the call.

Most of the time, when I look upon my fellow human beings, I see good people, witnesses all, men and women whose righteousness makes me ashamed of my failures, my cowardice, my incompetence. But there are other times, times of despair, when all I can see is the serpent who lures us into damnation. In those dark hours it seems that we are surrounded by merchants of death and dealers in murder who make the stuff of Auschwitz into something tantalizing, exciting, desirable, alluring. Idolatry is fashionable, slavery is commendable, and life is expendable. We slay one another with fixed formulas and ready answers, mouthing our lies to a tune that imparts to our emptiness a counterfeit sense of urgency. One look at Auschwitz ought to be enough for those who have eyes to see the deception of what we pass off in our institutions of higher learning as the highest truth. Auschwitz is the marketplace *par excellence,* where human beings themselves become the raw material for a machine whose sole purpose is the consumption of more human raw material.

"When I looked at the smoking chimneys of that factory," Ka-tzetnik once said to me, "I wondered what product it was producing. After all, a factory produces something, but here I could see nothing. Later I found out that while those chimneys smoked with their terrible flames, there was another fire being invented at Los Alamos."

As a people, the Jews signify the presence of God and truth in the world. The windows of the Temple were constructed not to let light in but to allow the light of the Holy One, blessed be He, to emanate into the world. So it is with the Jewish people. So it is intended for all people. Each human being is a bridge, a passageway to the holy and through which the holy enters the world and sanctifies life. The meaning of life may be found in the first utterance of Creation: Let there be light. The meaning of life is that we are not only to be a light unto the world, but we are to turn darkness into light, matter into spirit, wherever possible. Even when it seems impossible. Especially when it seems impossible.

But since the Jews are particularly chosen for this testimony, they are the first to be transformed from living spirit into dead matter. The spirituality of oneself is enhanced by serving the material needs of the other, by caring for the sick, feeding the hungry, and easing the suffering of the oppressed. But when I use the other human being to serve my own material ends, then I drain the world of spirit, of God, of all there is to hold dear. Each time we make another person into raw material to serve our own pleasure, whether that pleasure is political or sensual, we join the ranks of the builders of the death factory.

There are moments when I fear that the world has become one massive death factory, and that the schools intended to protect the holy have become training grounds for the production of more human raw material. As we are told in the Talmud, blessing does not belong to what can be weighed, measured, or counted. Why? Because the essence of the human being, created in the image of God, does not belong to what can be weighed, measured, or counted. He who makes human value, the value of a human being, into something determined by the scales of the marketplace, is an accomplice to Himmler and to all who would dismantle homes to make them into barracks and blocks.

Today I should go out to buy some gifts for my loved ones, look into some bookstores, and do some work in the library. I hope the library will prove more fruitful today than it did yesterday...

This trip to the Hebrew University Library has not been as productive as I had hoped, but I have engaged in other forms of "research" that could not be done in any library. I have sought out places in Poland where I had never been, and in Israel I have searched again, re-searched, places I had visited before but had not yet seen in this new light, this new darkness. I have looked upon the handiwork of the Angel of Death, the Angel with a Thousand Eyes, and he has left me with new eyes through which I may seek out and look upon life anew. Already I see new paths to pursue in my work. Gouri indicated that he would try to set up a meeting for me with a circle of Russian-Israeli writers. That would be of immense help. There, too, my vision has taken a new turn.

This journey, this pilgrimage, has given me a much deeper perspective on my so-called professional endeavors as a scholar. (I don't like that word, *professional*. It has come to indicate ways to avoid *professing* anything.) I have always made an effort to somehow address the truth in the things I study and write about. You cannot write, I have told myself, without seeking to write the truth. But I have been working as a Russian teacher, and I have been con-scious of a certain duty to write on things Russian and thus establish some kind of "reputation" as a Russian scholar.

I am about to complete a book, for example, on the motif of exile in modern Russian letters. I believe that such a book will have a larger contribution to make, one that goes far beyond the parameters of Russian studies. It has a strong Jewish element, since the problem of dwelling in the world is central to Jewish thought and therefore to the truth of human life. In fact, three of the main figures I examine in it are Jewish. Nevertheless, I confess with shame that the thought of advancing my career in Russian has entered my mind in connection with that book.

Now, however, I see that my work must assume an explicitly Jewish focus, regardless of any career concerns. Making a life involves too much time and energy to squander any of it on making a living. Or maybe the real task is to combine the two into a single pursuit. If I deal further with things "Russian," it will be with Russian Jews in their Jewishness, like this project I am trying to develop on Russian-Israeli authors. And my end will be not only to make a point about a topic but to bear witness to the truth that lends the topic its significance.

Many times, despite my warnings to myself, I have separated my writing from my inner wrestling, but now, perhaps beginning with this journal, I see it taking a new and deeper turn. When it is in service to the truth, when it is a medium of testimony, as it must be, the word is a portal to that interior where Within and Above become synonyms. Home, indeed, is made of such an interior. The responsibility of one human being to another and for another is a form of such an interiority. There can be no home, no dwelling in the world, without this interiority. To be in exile is to be exiled from the interior, adrift on a sea of indifference.

Since I left home nearly two weeks ago I have spent almost all of my time in silence. I have the feeling that these long hours of silence have been good for my words. This time of quietude has itself been a kind of research, a researching into silence and thus into meaning, or into the roots of meaning. After all, as Rebbe Levi Yitzhak of Berditchev* once pointed out, when God gave the Torah,

---

*Hasidic master, 1740-1809.

He gave not only the words but the silence between the words as well. Which is to say: when God gave the Torah, He joined together word and meaning.

The Torah is what distinguishes the silence of Sinai from the silence that preceded the Beginning, the silence of presence and plenitude from the silence of absence and chaos. The place where word and meaning join is a place of silence in the recesses of the soul opened up at Sinai. That hidden depth is revealed in the space between two: between man and man, between man and God, *adam l'adam, adam la-Makom.* In an offering of all that lies within, each manifests to the other the name of the Nameless One, the Name hidden in all the names of the forgotten others, the Name buried beneath a mountain of ash that rivals the mountain Sinai.

Mount Sinai inaugurated an age that lasted for three thousand years. Now, in our own time, the mountain at Majdanek has inaugurated another age. Now it is from the dizzying heights of that dreaded mountain that we must find a way to utter and a way to hear the utterance of the one word spoken at Sinai: *Anochi,* I Am, with the *Am* couched in the *I,* and not separate from it. For the *Am* of the *I* is the *You* : to say "I am" is to declare "You are." And since God alone can say *I,* it is the *Anochi* of God that makes possible the revelation of the You. In the word spoken by God, therefore, lie all words ever said and yet to be said between one human being and another, between man and God. And through that word I must seek my brother, both living and dead, in every handful of ashes.

I think I realize now why the *Kaddish* is so often recited in the synagogue, why the memory of the deceased is so central to Jewish life. If we should lose our memory of those who have gone before us, who have come out of Egypt and therefore made possible the blessings we enjoy, then we would lose our own souls. The soul is made of memory, and memory is made of loved ones who have returned to the bosom of the Most High. I see that from now on I must stand for the *Kaddish* and place myself among those who mourn and thus among those who remember.

11 SIVAN 5751

Jerusalem, 24 May 1991

THIS MORNING, IN A WAY that I have never experienced it before, I feel the peace that this City of Peace signifies. The *Tefillah*, the daily Prayer, closes with an affirmation of the peace that only God can bring. It is the *shalom*, the *shalem*, that means wholeness, the one genuine wholeness that lies in the relation to the Holy One which alone can bring peace to every other relation. No one created in the image of God can be hale and whole without the relation to God. As far as the geography of that relation goes, I have never sensed it so strongly as I do here and now in Jerusalem. There is tension in the city, yes. There is strife. In fact, I just heard two explosions, but I have no idea what they were or where they came from. Nonetheless there is peace, because there is proximity to the holiness of the Holy One.

I do not see how anyone can be at peace without this proximity. Asleep, perhaps, but not at peace. The peace of Jerusalem is a state of profound awareness and wakefulness, a sense of the connectedness of all things, a sense of the oneness and the wholeness that the word *shalom* conveys. It is the oneness with oneself that arises only in a oneness with others and is therefore the most essential aspect of dwelling. To dwell is to be at peace.

Without the peace of this place called Jerusalem, no one can create a home in any place on the planet. The Temple of stone from which light emanated into the world is gone, but I see now that the Temple of light abides. It persists through those human beings, both Jews and Gentiles, who turn darkness into light; who embody the characteristics of modesty, generosity, and lovingkindness; who are witnesses and messengers testifying to the dearness of the other human being. These are the remnants of the Temple of Jerusalem.

And in this world a remnant is a lot.

I have finished reading all but the last few pages of Rambam's *Guide for the Perplexed*. These last pages deal with how we are to worship God. After I complete my reading of the *Guide*, I shall take up a book called *Biblical Images* by Rabbi Steinsaltz. I think it is an appropriate selection for the rest of my stay in Israel, as well as for my return home. After all, these are the images of people born in this land, in some cases people who spoke with the Holy One Himself. Therefore they are people who create the possibility of a home.

Having endured these encounters with Auschwitz and Jerusalem, I am more convinced than ever that there is a definitive connection between the meaning of life and the meaning of home. If it is God's will that I return, then when I go home I shall go to a place where I have never been. At the end of this expedition, I shall return to where I started and know the place for the first time. Like the purpose of every journey, of every pilgrimage, the real aim of this one was not to visit the camps or to go to the Wall but to return home.

Martin Buber once said that the Good is that which leads you homeward. Like the Good, my home and family choose me before I have chosen anything. Indeed, I do not have the freedom to choose unless I have thus been chosen. Freedom cannot mean being free to choose between good and evil, since that would suggest that a person is free even in the midst of evil. Only he is free who has a home, for those who have a home are among the chosen. And those who choose create a place to dwell.

To be in exile is to be unchosen, or rather to refuse the choice that comes in the light of having already been chosen. Jerusalem signifies the dwelling that transpires within the home, because Jerusalem signifies this chosenness and the choosing that such dwelling demands. Thus every road homeward, at least for the Jew, passes through Jerusalem. Moving in the other direction, all the roads that take us into exile lead to Auschwitz.

In the task of dwelling, however, it is not enough to have a home. For having a home comes only with providing a place for the other human being to dwell. In his *Menorat HaMaor (Lamp of the Light)* the fourteenth-century Spanish Jew, Israel ibn al-Nakawa, tells us that the leaders of certain Jewish communities in France would have their coffins made of the boards from the tables they used to feed the poor. This, he says, was to show that no matter how high we may reach, we can take nothing from this world into the next except the good we have done and the compassion we have shown toward others. That is what dwelling is about. It is a matter that concerns our lives not only in this world but in the *olam ha-ba*, the world to come, as well.

The greatness of this Land of Israel lies in its primary aim of providing a home for all Jews, and without Israel no Jew can be at home anywhere. Even Israel, however, has its dark side. This is not the homeland established by the Messiah, and so even here the homelessness of the other human being is a blight upon the land. Perhaps this is something that only the Messiah can resolve.

For the coming of the Messiah will mean not the end of the world but the end of the wandering in the wilderness of homelessness, and that will come only when the Word and the Truth of the Holy One, blessed be He, are inscribed upon the hearts of all human beings, Jew and non-Jew alike. But it is the Jew who must make it happen. That is what being a Jew means. And that is what makes the Jew *other,* even to himself. Especially to himself. For the Messiah will come on the day when every Jew is a Jew in all his or her Jewishness. On that day he will *have* to come. He will have no choice. For he will have been chosen by God's Chosen....

Friday afternoon. I think I see now what this peace that pervades me might be. It is the peace of the approaching Sabbath. You can sense it in Jerusalem more powerfully than anywhere else on the globe. More than "in the air," it is in the earth, in the people, in the soul. It steals over you without your realizing it at first. Then it reveals to you the truth of Jerusalem's proximity to the "inner spheres of holiness," as Rabbi Steinsaltz puts it. It is true: what we are, as Jews, lies very much in what the Sabbath means to us. For the Sabbath means creation and liberation, home and family, the unity of God and humanity—everything that being Jewish means.

For me, the only thing missing from the peace and the wholeness of this Sabbath is what is most essential to every Sabbath of my life: Gerri, Miriam, and Rachel.

With the coming of the Sabbath, my renewed sense of gratitude runs even deeper. And, on this Sabbath, the dearness of my family is all the more pronounced, precisely because of their absence—or rather because of their presence made all the more urgent by their absence. As the Sabbath Bride makes her way into Jerusalem, I am reminded all the more of the new and unimagined love I have found for my own bride.

Last week I spent the Sabbath in Warsaw along the

frayed edges of a broken branch.

This week I am in the midst of the roots of the Tree of Life.

And, here in Jerusalem, by the light of the Sabbath that comes with the fading light of the day, I behold the love of the Holy One whose divine light makes all love what it is. This love and this light I shall take to my wife. This love and this light she brings to me, even when we are at a distance from one another, just as the Sabbath lends its light and its substance to those days that are distant and distinct from it.

It is time for me to leave off writing for a day. It is time for *Kiddush*.

Why hasn't Gouri called?

13 SIVAN 5751

Jerusalem, 26 May 1991

I SPENT A SHABBAT overflowing with the rest and contemplative repose of *menuchah,* as one can spend it only in Jerusalem. Not long after rising early in the morning I walked to the synagogue on the Givat Ram campus, but it was closed. So I stood outside the entrance to the synagogue and said my Sabbath prayers.

Much of the day I spent reading the *Siddur,* the *Pirkei Avot (Ethics of the Fathers),* and Steinsaltz's *Biblical Images.* Every word spoke to me and revealed to me in a new light, in a Sabbath light, the essence of the path before me, the nature of my errors, and the profound need and assignation of love, caring, and responsibility. There were moments when everything seemed so simple and so clear to me, moments that belong only to the Sabbath. Just as the words we speak throughout the day take on their meaning from the words of prayer we utter each morning, so do all the days of the week derive their substance from the Day of Rest.

The moments of revelation came from more than just the words I read. As I walked about this beautiful campus on a hill overlooking the Knesset, I saw several families enjoying and rejoicing in the peace of the Sabbath afternoon.

There was one little boy in particular whom I remember. He was climbing a statue of birds in flight, as if he were about to take flight himself. Watching him at play, I too had the sensation of soaring, released from the forces of gravity that weigh on us during the week. I felt that I had been freed from many of the manacles that I have forged for myself and have imposed on my loved ones. This Shabbat—for the first time and by the grace of *HaShem*—I was able to leave off with the cares of the world, if only for a short while, and approach that reflective tranquility which distinguishes *menuchah*.

My second Sabbath away from home has brought me closer to home. Seeing the families out for their walks with their little children, I felt both a longing for and a deeper closeness to my own family. I was alone, but I was not exactly lonely, as I am now. For I experienced a nearness to that which draws one human being nigh to another, beginning with husband and wife, parent and child.

Meanwhile, not all the Israelis were out for a walk with their families on this Shabbat. Many were hard at work. But their work was sanctioned by the rabbinical authorities in the name of *pikuach nefesh*, the religious imperative which tells us that we must violate the observances of the Sabbath if it means saving a human life. For this Shabbat Israel undertook Operation Solomon, the airlift of nearly fifteen thousand Ethiopian Jews from a country torn by civil war. As I was drawing closer to a sense of home and dwelling on its meaning, the Israelis were providing a new home and a new hope of life for these fifteen thousand Jews.

The operation involved forty sorties of IAF and El Al aircraft, including one flight that carried a world-record 1,080 passengers. An army bus driver commented that they could not have done it with "pudgy Russians and Israelis" carrying five suitcases in each hand. "They are thin, these Ethiopians," he said. "They are hungry." And they are grateful as only the hungry know how to be. Looking at the television news reports, I realized that I had never seen a group of people beaming with such gratitude. They did not know how to use the elevators in the buildings where they have been taken. They even had to be shown how to operate the toilets. Primitive? Perhaps. But how wonderfully *human* they are in their gratitude!

Known as Beta-Yisrael, or the Falashim, no one knows exactly where or how the Ethiopian Jews arose. Having lived in the hills of Ethiopia since the time of the Babylonian Exile, the Beta-Yisrael have no knowledge of the Talmud and turn almost exclusively to the Torah for their way of life—a situation that has led the Rabbinate to insist that they receive instruction in the faith.

Some sources regard them as the descendants of proselytes. For the last five hundred years, however, many rabbis have identified the Falashim with the Lost Tribe of Dan, one of the ten tribes driven out of Israel by the Assyrians in 722 B.C.E. The renowned fifteenth-century rabbi from Egypt, David ibn abu Zimra (known as Radbaz), declared them to be the descendants of that tribe. His ruling was the basis for the recognition of the Falashim as Jews by the chief Sephardic Rabbi of Israel five hundred years later.

Whatever their origins may be, legends surrounding the Falashim abound. One tale, which comes from the Falashim themselves, has it that they are the children of Moses, who reigned as king in Ethiopia after he fled from Egypt. Josephus, the first-century Jewish historian, in fact maintains that Moses took over the rule of Ethiopia upon entering the land at the head of the Egyptian army. Other Ethiopian Jews claim that the Beta-Yisrael are the offspring of King Solomon and the Queen of Sheba; indeed, most scholars believe that Ethiopia was part of the kingdom ruled by the Queen. According to still another version, they were among the Jews of the Exodus who failed to make it across the parted waters of the Red Sea.

This time, however, they made it across, "on wings of eagles," as it were. Israel is alive with excitement and an eagerness to serve its Ethiopian brothers and sisters. I love the commitment of this country to all Jews who are in need of a haven, even when providing a haven is most difficult. The problems created by the massive immigration of the Russian Jews are immense. And yet there was not a moment's hesitation to come to the aid of the fifteen thousand Falashim. There is nothing else like it on the face of the earth.

Israel offers no excuses in the way of immigration quotas where saving the lives of Jews is concerned. When it comes to fellow Jews, there is a real brotherhood here, one that exemplifies what other countries—Christian, Moslem, and otherwise—should emulate.

How many of the Arab countries, for example, have offered their land as a home, or even as a temporary refuge, for the Palestinians? Yes, when it comes to their fellow Jews, the Israelis come out with open arms. But I wonder: can there ever be a genuine brotherhood as long as we do not view non-Jews too as our brothers?

Seeing this miraculous concern for life, I am reminded of the Tree of Life that Judaism signifies. Yes, most of the Israelis are secular Jews, but here even the secular Jews embrace many of the highest values of Judaism, sometimes despite themselves. Seeing the truth of Judaism transformed into flesh and blood, I realize some of the error in the thought of many thinkers whose ideas I once embraced. The tension between faith and reason that characterizes the likes of, say, Pascal and Kierkegaard or Dostoevsky and Shestov misses the point. These existential thinkers are correct in their desire to bring the life we must live to the ideas we ponder. Truth, Kierkegaard rightly argues, consists not in knowing the truth but in being the truth. And, as these thinkers have maintained, each in his own way, knowing the truth lies in knowing God.

But the essential thing missing from their thought, the thing essential to Jewish thought, is the idea that knowing God entails a *responsibility* for the other human being. Dostoevsky was close in his assertion that each is responsible for all, but he was not able to remove this notion from a Christian dogma that excludes all who do not directly embrace it. Unlike the Jews, who believe that there is a place in the *olam ha-ba* for the righteous of all faiths, these Christians generally maintain that the hereafter belongs only to the Christians.

And I believe that these thinkers have a disregard for the material side of life that can prove to be dangerous to human being. Our purpose in life, as Kazantzakis has said, is to turn matter into spirit, into love and joy. And how do we do that? By attending to the material need of the other human being, just as the Israelis served that need yesterday, on the Sabbath, when they opened their doors to the Falashim. The Jewish soul flourished in its attendance to the needs of those thin bodies.

I was hungry, and you fed me, said the Jew Jesus. I was thirsty, and you gave me drink. I was naked, and you clothed me. I was in prison, and you came to comfort me. What he did not say is: I was a sinner, and you saved my soul. Jesus was a part of the Jewish Tree of Life, and there was almost nothing in his message on life that does not have its reverberations in the Torah. Indeed, nearly all of his teachings can be found in the teachings of the Sages—in the Talmud, the *Mechilta*, the *Pirkei* d'Rabbi Eliezer, the *Pesikta* of Rabbi Kahana, the Midrash, the *En Yaakov.* Judah Halevi, in fact, claims that Jesus was a disciple of Rabbi Joshua ben Perahyah, from the school of Hillel.

Can there be any doubt that the Jew from Nazareth

would weep bitterly at the sight of what the Christians have made of him? Can those who have nailed so many of his fellow Jews to the cross possibly be among his followers? I remember that at Majdanek, Auschwitz, and elsewhere crucifixions were one means of execution. And just a kilometer or so from where I am sitting right now is the Valley of the Cross, the place from which the Romans took the tree upon which they crucified the Nazarene Jew.

More later. Right now I have to check out of Beit Belgia and move to the Maiersdorf House on Mount Scopus....

In another of her innumerable acts of kindness, Liat has just dropped me off at the Maiersdorf House on the Mount Scopus campus of Hebrew University. She took me to see the synagogue here, one of the few in the world that does not have an eastern wall, since it is east of the Temple Mount. On its western wall is a large window that looks out onto the Mount where the Temple twice stood. As I gazed out the window that framed this amazing sight, I found the thought of worshiping here every day overwhelming.

Sitting here even now, in my room on the fifth floor, I have a magnificent view of the Mount, the Old City, the New City—all of Jerusalem. I don't think there is any view anywhere in the world more beautiful than this. I could sit here for hours staring at this city full of peace and strife, joy and sadness, love and hatred—all the elements of the human soul and the divine spirit. From this room I can see the center of the forces that shape the world that extends far, far into every direction. From here I can see the center of the forces that rattle the heavenly spheres themselves. What keeps me from fainting in a swoon, I do not know.

For it is with this sight before me that I have just spoken on the phone with Eliyah and Yehiel De-Nur. Yehiel is the Holocaust survivor and novelist known as Ka-tzetnik 135633. Eliyah is herself a poet and one of the most remarkable women I have ever known. She once told me that many years ago she had a vision of Jesus. Speaking to her in Yiddish, he told her to go on a forty-day fast. At the end of the fast she saw a doctor and was diagnosed with cancer. The doctor told her that if she had not gone on the fast, she would certainly have died.

This time, however, she received no help from a vision. She just told me, in a tone of affirming defiance, that she is helping a seventeen-year-old boy in Jerusalem with his fight against cancer. Then Yehiel came on the phone and told me that Eliyah is dying of inoperable lung cancer. That is how this saintly woman "deals with" death and dying: by helping another. No denial. No anger. No bargaining. None of the clinically determined stages of dying. Yehiel confessed that he is taking it much worse than she, and I could hear a terrible distress in his voice. He said that he needs someone to hug and that he would like that someone to be me.

Me? I could not understand this. How could I merit such words from a man who, I believe, is surely among the *Lamed Vav,* the Thirty-Six Just Men whose righteousness prevents God from destroying the world? For me this would be a gift from the Holy One Himself. But it is a gift that comes with unspeakable sadness. Why does it seem that gifts from God are so often like that? I cannot help weeping for her, for him, for the world.

I look up and see a huge crack in the wall of my room. It is like the crack in the universe that I am sensing right now. They have tried to plaster it, but it has the look of a wound that will not heal. Outside my window the wind is howling. It has the sound of a deeply mournful lament. *Eichah!*

These last two weeks have been made of long hours of one extreme after another. It is taking its toll on me. I have to gather together all my concentration, every ounce of what energy I have left, and strain to focus my will in order to go on. I mustn't lose it now. I mustn't let go, no matter how great the temptation to curl up in a fetal position and slip into the inviting sleep of forgetfulness.

Lives are at stake. More lives than I can know have been placed in my hands. I can feel their weight with my every movement. Already I sense that one of them is fading away. Eliyah is dying. And Yehiel survived two years in Auschwitz, two Auschwitz-years, only to live to see the one he loves most deeply of all going through this ordeal. He tells the story of their amazing love in his novel *Phoenix Over the Galilee.*

He wrote his first book *Sunrise Over Hell* over forty-five years ago, as he lay dying in an Italian hospital, unable to eat any food. It was the testimony he had promised the dead that he would offer if he should escape the death camp. Knowing that he was on the edge of death, he asked for writing materials so that he might keep his vow. Two weeks later the work was finished, and Yehiel was on his way to a miraculous recovery.

When he handed the manuscript to a Jewish soldier for safe keeping, the soldier noticed that the author's name did not appear on it. He asked the man still dressed in the prisoner's stripes of Auschwitz, "Who shall I say wrote it?"

And Yehiel answered, "Who wrote it? *They* wrote it! Put *their* name on it: Ka-tzetnik!"

And so he took on the names and the souls of the dead gathered into this one name. They eclipsed his *I* and took over his voice.

A few months later Yehiel was living in Tel-Aviv, where he and Eliyah now have their home. He spent his days on one park bench and his nights on another. Meanwhile his book—the first Holocaust novel, the first testimony, to be published—was in every Jewish household. But no one, not even the publisher, knew who its author was. Years later his children read the works of Ka-tzetnik in the schools they attended and did not know that their father was the author of those books. Israel has set up a literary award known as the Ka-tzetnik Prize, but the man for whom the award is named has never appeared at an award ceremony.

The young Eliyah read *Sunrise Over Hell* and spent a year trying to find the man who wrote it. She went to the publisher, who told her that if the author had wanted his name to be known, then he would have given his name. The man was too embarrassed to tell her that even he, the book's publisher, did not know who its author was. Somehow she finally found him, and she has been with him ever since, enduring with him all the horror of his effort to find his way back to life. There were times when he would disappear for months on end and then return with another book he had written. For thirty years he did not sleep at night because of the nightmares that haunted him. Finally, Eliyah took him to Holland, where she saw him through weeks of therapy that ultimately cured him of the nightmares.

And now her life is ebbing away before his eyes. And he needs someone to hug. And he asked me to come tomorrow and to be that someone. How can I possibly be worthy of this? Ten days ago I was on the site where he spent two eternal years of his life. And *he* wants to embrace *me*! Everything is upside down. I don't understand.

And the Russian Jews continue to escape to this Land where they do not know the language, and the Israelis fly the Falashim out of Ethiopia, and the young men and women all around me, hardly more than children, scurry about the halls of the Mount Scopus campus, and the rabbis issue their condemnations, and the survivors of the Hurban die off one by one, and the *Kotel* raises up its silent cry to the silence of the Heaven of heavens, and the ovens of the Kingdom of Night coldly cast their shadows over the face of the earth. Down the hall is the Hecht Synagogue with the stand from which the Torah scrolls are read facing the Temple Mount. Somehow it is all connected. Somehow I am tied to it all. But how?

I cannot get over the thought that, if it is God's will that I see Eliyah tomorrow, it will probably be the last time that I ever see this woman who is famous throughout the land for her lovingkindness. We never know which time will be the last time we see one another. Therefore, when we part, let it be with words of kindness and compassion. The last look into the eyes, the last touch of the hand, the last embrace—let it all be filled with love.

On the wall of my room hangs a painting of Abraham in the midst of his terrifying dream. Did he see in his vision what I have seen the remnants of?

14 SIVAN 5751

Jerusalem, 27 May 1991

LAST NIGHT LIAT AND Itamar invited me over for an excellent meal. They also invited two Russian immigrants who are now their neighbors. The Russians speak no English and very little Hebrew, and Liat thought they might enjoy speaking to someone who knew some Russian. So I chatted with them for a couple of hours in their native tongue. They are young, in their mid-30s, and they have a four-year-old son. He is a computer programmer, and she is a pianist. He seems to have found a position for himself, but she has come to a land where there are thousands of excellent pianists out of work. She was especially interested in the United States, indicating that she was much more interested in learning English than in studying Hebrew.

They never had any exposure to things religious in the Soviet Union. Only a few years ago it was a crime to even study Hebrew in that country. Subsequently they are not very religious, but they are very courageous. Think of it: you leave behind your every possession, the accumulations of a lifetime. With your child in hand, you say farewell to mother and father, sister and brother, and set out for a place you have never been, a place whose language, whose every aspect, is completely alien to you. They still have family in Moscow, and they told me that their family is still in danger, as is every Jew who lives there. The nationalist, anti-Semitic movement known as *Pamyat*, for example, requires its new members to submit the names and addresses of at least five Jewish families.

Looking into the eyes of these Jews sitting before me, I could see the eyes of all those Russian Jews in search of a home. The eyes were Jewish, yet they were unsure of their new land, still not at home with the Hebrew tongue. They are here, and yet they are elsewhere, stranded along the margins of the word. Their language holds them at the border of the land, and from there they search for the key that will enable them to enter.

And so they live without knowing, or even having the illusion of knowing, what the next day might bring. They live without knowing what will become of the family they left behind or the child they brought with them. To have a home is to have a reasonable notion of what might become of your children. Home is the hope of a life and a place for your children. I have immense admiration for these people and the fortitude they exemplify. Few people I have known are capable of what these Russian Jews have undertaken. And I have a deep compassion and sympathy for their plight. Perhaps if they can come to themselves, find themselves, as Jews, then they may find a home in Israel.

Liat, in keeping with her Jewish essence, has been very generous and very kind to them. She bought furniture for them and had them over to her home for a Passover Seder, probably the first Seder they had ever been to. Just so, she has been amazingly kind to me, to my daughters, and to my wife. This morning she is coming to pick me up and take me to the bus station. Once I get to Tel-Aviv, I must call Yehiel and Eliyah.

❧

Tel-Aviv, 27 May 1991

I am sitting in my room at the Tal Hotel, just a block from the Mediterranean Sea. Looking upon those waters, I am reminded of the ancient vessels that sailed this sea and the sailors they carried. What did they seek beyond the horizon of those depths? These are the waters that Judah Halevi traveled on his way to Zion. As he rode his ship, he wrote:

> The face of the waters and the face of the heavens, the
>   infinity of the sea,
> The infinity of night, are grown pure, are made clear,
> And the sea appears as a firmament—
> Then are they two seas bound up together;
> And between them is my heart, a third sea,
> Lifting up ever anew my waves of praise.

I too felt waves of praise rise up from within me when I spoke to Gerri last night on the phone. She called while I was at Liat's house. Once again I was relieved and thankful to hear her voice, to hear that my children are well, to hear that I have a home.

And yet I think that it is only from here, in Israel, that I have realized that I do have a home, that I have caught some small glimpse of what having a home means. It is a realization that has come to me by looking upon the world through the eyes of those, both living and dead, who are homeless. Therefore my debt to them becomes greater still. Not only do I approach my self and my soul by way of the other, but it is also by way of the other that I return home. Without my wife and my children, of course, none of this is possible or even thinkable. Nothing is possible. The thought is at once exhilarating and terrifying.

I just got off the phone with Yehiel. I am to see him and

Eliyah at five-thirty this afternoon. Yehiel told me that Eliyah has had a bad day today. For the dying, good and bad are measured by degrees of suffering. Waves of praise? Waves of pain. I had thought that I might tape our conversation, but now I don't think so. There are times when certain words should not be taken down by a machine. Some things are lost when they are recorded.

It reminds me of what the Baal Shem once said to one of his disciples who was writing down everything that came from the mouth of the Master: "There is nothing of me in what you have written. I said one thing, you heard another and wrote a third."

In an hour or so I'll begin my walk to their home. I think it is around five kilometers, the distance I walked from the Treblinka train stop to the site of the death camp....

I am back from my talk with Eliyah and Yehiel. My head is swimming. My soul is drowning. Eliyah had risen from her bed and from her pain to spend just a few minutes sitting with me. There was the smile of a saint on her face and the sadness of a dying soul in her words, or rather beneath her words. Her cancer was discovered only a month ago, just a day or two after she and Yehiel had written to me that they were looking forward to my visit.

"It is the third time this has happened to me," she explained. "Whenever someone new enters my life, someone I love, I pay through the nose for it." Then she paused to let her moment of anger subside. I was wondering whom she was talking about, when she looked hard into my eyes and explained, "You know that I love you, don't you?"

Once again I reeled, as I have day after day. How can I merit this? How can I ever live up to it?

Then she asked me about my conversion and wanted to know how it had changed my reading of the Scriptures. In her profound wisdom, she understands that a person cannot undergo such a transformation of body and soul without the message he receives also being transformed. I told her that now, as I study the Torah, I am no longer engaged in the investigation of a religious topic or even of a religious text, as though it were something that lies outside of me. Now, when I study the Torah, I am engaged in a prayer to God and an address from God, through which I seek my own soul. Now, when I study the Torah, I take on a responsibility in which I must answer to and for the other human being, in the light of what has been given to me through the Holy Word.

Then she picked up a book about Teresa of Avila. "My favorite saint," she said, and I recalled that Teresa is the favorite saint of my closest friend outside of my family, a man named Luis Cortest. Like Eliyah, he is one of the few people I have known who has a genuine sense of the sanctity and the responsibility that lend life its meaning. It was no coincidence.

She turned to a passage that came to her mind as she listened to my remarks about my conversion. It said that God has given us two commandments: to love Him with all our heart, all our soul, and all that we are. And to love our fellow human being. The love for our fellow human being must happen first, read Eliyah. We do not know how to love God, but we know how to love our neighbor. And loving our neighbor turns out to be precisely how we are to love God. For if we love our neighbor, then God will reward us by increasing the depth of our love for Him.

Hearing this, I was reminded of the saying in the Talmud that the reward for performing a *mitzvah* is that we perform another *mitzvah*. The reward for being good is that we become good. Can there be any greater reward in life?

Eliyah told me that she had wanted to be like Teresa, to imitate her in her righteousness. "And then one day," she said, "I realized something: I can be like Teresa only by not being like Teresa—by being who I am, not by being who she is." Life, in other words, is not a matter of imitation, even if the one imitated is a saint. Rather, it is a matter of response.

Again the utterance of the Hasidic Sage, Rebbe Zusya, ran through my mind: "When I stand before the Celestial Tribunal, I shall not be asked, 'Why weren't you Abraham?' or 'Why weren't you Moses?' I shall be asked, 'Why weren't you Zusya?'"

And so it was that every time she spoke, in her words I heard the echoes of the wise.

I am so weary. It is very late. I shall have to continue this tomorrow.

15 SIVAN 5751

Tel-Aviv, 28 May 1991

MY DREAMS LAST NIGHT were filled with images from my talk with Eliyah and Yehiel, her eyes overflowing with lovingkindness, his ridden with fear....

It was a forty-five minute walk from my hotel to their apartment. Strolling through the streets of Tel-Aviv—up Nordau, left on Ibn Gavirol, right on Yehudah Ha-Maccabee to Weizmann—I almost had the feeling that I had left Israel. I had to remind myself that Israel is not Jerusalem, that Jerusalem is in a category by itself. But so is Israel. And, perhaps in a way, Israel is Jerusalem. Certainly Israel cannot be what it is without Jerusalem and the holiness that emanates from the heart of that city, from the Western Wall and the Temple Mount. When I think of Gerri's love for Jerusalem, I love her all the more.

I arrived at their apartment at the appointed time, and Yehiel greeted me at the door. As always, the number on his arm was covered with a long-sleeved shirt. He hesitated for a moment, a bit puzzled: he did not recognize me.

"David, you are so different," he said.

Was it the fuller, grayer beard perhaps? No. The *kipah*?

No, it wasn't that. He could not put his finger on it, but he insisted that I had changed dramatically. I wanted to tell him that it was the ashes that now covered me, that my eyes had been changed by what they had seen. But I merely smiled at his moment of confusion. Then he smiled too and put his arms around me, tattoo and all.

Eliyah was sitting in a chair next to the door. As her husband was trying to figure out how I had changed, she insisted to him that I had not changed a bit. Eliyah has a way of seeing through the ashes.

But she had changed. Although it was only two years since I last saw her, she looked ten years older. Her face was marked with pain and sickness. And yet it beamed with love.

She apologized for being unable to hug me. (Apologizing to *me!* It was so like her. Still, I do not understand.) Even her loose clothing was painful next to her body. But she asked me to kiss her on the cheek, and I did. We talked for only a few minutes—about her illness and my conversion, about Teresa of Avila, Elie Wiesel, Martin Buber. Eliyah loves Buber's tales of the Hasidim. During the Gulf War she was in Haifa, and Yehiel was out of the country. She said that almost every night, as the Iraqi missiles were raining down, she would call Yehiel and read to him from Buber's tales of the Hasidim. Yehiel, on the other hand, said that he prefers Wiesel's approach to Hasidism.

"I like Elie's *Souls on Fire*," he told me. "It is written from the inside, from the viewpoint of a Hasid."

Recalling that Buber had ceased wearing *talit* and *tefill-in* at the age of fourteen, I agreed. There is a certain love, a flaming passion, in Wiesel's approach to Hasidism, something that can come only from within the trains laden with a cargo destined for the death factory.

At that point Eliyah rose to return to her bed. Holding her dressing gown out from her body, she looked at me, smiled, and sang, "We'll meet again, don't know where, don't know when." Somehow I managed to restrain my tears. Would I ever see her again? Almost certainly not. At least not in this world. Her eyes had the look of one last look. They haunt me still.

And yet I answered her, "Yes, we'll meet again." The insistent line from the Amidah ran through my mind: "Blessed art Thou who raises the dead."

"There is no one like her in all of Israel," Yehiel said to me after she had left the room. "She is always doing so much. Even now, despite her condition, she goes to help the boy dying of cancer in Jerusalem. She just..."

He did not finish his sentence. The grief was too much for him. Trying to change the subject (and yet with Yehiel the subject is always the same), he asked me about my stay in Poland, and I told him very briefly about the places I had been. He was quite familiar with that country, for he was born there, the grandnephew of the great Hasidic Rabbi Nachman of Bratzlav. I could see, however, that he needed to talk, and so for the next two hours I listened intensely to his every word and answered his questions as best I could.

The first thing he wanted to know was whether any of the wooden blocks are still standing at Birkenau, whether they were as he had described them in his books. It was as if he were not quite sure that they had ever existed, as if he were trying to verify for himself that it was not all a horrible nightmare, that he had not made it up. As oblivion is tied to exile, so is memory tied to redemption; but what if the memory is an illusion? Somehow it reminded me of Mr. Blum's search for some sign that his own past had been there.

Yes, Yehiel, I assured him, the plank beds are there in the blocks, just as you described them. Yes, the stone oven runs down the middle of the block. Yes, opposite the tracks where the Jews were unloaded and selected for death stand the blocks made from the bricks of the village of Birkenau. You did not make it up, Yehiel. You are not insane. (Or are you?) Yes, the words *Arbeit Macht Frei* are still there. It is all there. And yet, of course, it is not.

Yehiel was uncertain about the value of setting up Auschwitz as a place for visitors. He did not know whether this tourist attraction could add anything to the testimony of survivors like himself. He truly did not know. Can anyone point to these structures surrounded by thick grass, these places of torture and death made into exhibit halls, and declare, "This is Auschwitz"? How can it be? During the two years he spent as a Musselman, he said, he saw the blocks, he saw the SS, he saw the crematorium, the babies fed into the ovens, yet, in a way, he did not see it.

"There was no consciousness, no thought," he explained. "But the eyes were filming it. The brain was filing it. Later, in my books, in Holland, it came out."

One day he was being marched toward the forest outside the camp with a group of Jews. They were to be shot. But he slipped away from the group and escaped into the woods. On that day in January 1945 the Nazis were in the process of abandoning the camp to the Russians. They fled after shooting the last of the Jews that they could round up to be shot. After they had gone, Yehiel walked through the concentration camp Auschwitz. Nothing. He walked through the crematorium. Silence. And he kept walking. Jumping onto trains and horse-drawn carts, he made his way from Poland to Italy, completely unconscious of everything that passed before him or happened to him.

The book that he wrote in an Italian hospital while on the edge of death, *Sunrise Over Hell*, is now the topic of an essay contest that the tenth-grade students of Israel enter each year. The three students who write the best essays are awarded a three-year scholarship at the Hebrew University. Yehiel has been asked repeatedly to attend the award ceremony for these students. He has been asked to present

other awards given in his name to professional writers—
Herman Wouk, for example. But he cannot bring himself
to do it. It would create the illusion that *they,* after all, had
not been the author of his books and thus belie the author's name, Ka-tzetnik, that appears on those works. It
would be a recognition of one survivor at the expense of
the dead, a benefit derived from the blood of a million
and a half children.

"Eliyah tells me," he said, "that I should go and speak to
teachers in their seminars, talk with them, answer their
questions. I know she is right, and I say, 'Yes, you are
right.' But for some reason I cannot do it. I don't know
why."

"Perhaps," I suggested to him, "it is because you feel
that you cannot speak for the dead. Perhaps you feel that
you should avoid the impression that they did not die."

He nodded, but his face was still filled with doubt.

He went on to talk about his most recent book, his one
work of nonfiction, *Shivitti.* Its Hebrew title means "I have
set myself before Thee," from the line in the Sixteenth
Psalm: "I have set myself before Thee always, O Lord."

"It was just like the first book," he told me. "Only the
first one was about Harry Preleshnik, the man who was *in*
Auschwitz. This one is *Auschwitz* itself."

Yes, I was thinking to myself as he spoke, it is true. The
last time I was here in Israel, I visited Yehiel and told him
about my interest in the novels that dealt with the Shoah
and in his novels in particular. He listened to me for a few
minutes and then suddenly went to his desk and pulled out
the manuscript of the English translation of *Shivitti.*

"Take it!" he said. "Take it! You will read it. You will
bring it back to me tomorrow. Take it! This is the key!"

I had never met him before, and yet here was this man
entrusting to me the manuscript of a book into which he
had poured the life's blood of his soul. I took it back to
Jerusalem that night and spent long, sleepless hours plow-

ing through its pages. As I read the manuscript, I felt I was being drawn toward the invisible inside of the Death Camp as such. I was undone at every word of those visions that rival the visions of Ezekiel himself.

Like his first book, this last one was written during two and a half weeks of unconsciousness of anything else. Yehiel rose from his chair and acted out for me how he came to write the book's first words. It had been ten years since he had undergone four LSD therapy sessions in Holland to rid himself of thirty years of nightmares. The doctor wanted him to go through a fifth session, but he refused. I think he might have been afraid of what he would see, afraid, perhaps, that he would never come out of it. During the next ten years, he said, he had thought day and night about how he might get it down on paper.

But the first words would not come.

Then one day *Shivitti* happened, like a fifth therapy session that he could not avoid.

"I was sleeping on the floor here," he said, pointing to the carpet in front of me. Why on the floor? Perhaps the dreams were more manageable there? I don't know. I didn't ask. I looked on and listened to his accented English, a language he is reluctant to speak, he says, since it is the language of those who abandoned the Jews.

"Eliyah was not here. She was away. I was lying here, it was morning, and it came to me. I rose up and was standing here at this desk. Reaching over with one hand, I wrote, 'This is the first session with Mr. De-Nur.' The first words were out.

"I pulled over a chair and started writing, writing, conscious of nothing else. Then I noticed that I could no longer see, and I turned on this lamp. And so I went on and on. When it was finished, I don't know how I knew it was finished. I didn't know how long I had been writing. I saw that the blanket was still on the floor. Then I noticed, suddenly, the things on the desk, the picture of Eliyah, and somehow, I knew that it was finished, because now I could see these other things.

"I have no memory of eating or drinking anything, no memory of getting up for anything, going to the toilet, nothing. I am sure I did these things. I must have. But there is no memory. Just the writing for two and a half weeks. That is all I remember.

"And, yes, one other thing: I remember the cry of a child, a neighbor's child. It was a cry of life. Perhaps it was the one thing that enabled me to keep my hold on life, like the spark that sustained me when I was writing my first book in the hospital. In each case I was in a race with death."

When he mentioned the cry of the child, I thought of the names of the children chanted in the Children's Memorial at Yad Vashem. Those children would no longer cry out to anyone. No longer were they a lifeline for the world. Whose voice will save us now?

Perhaps the voice of Ka-tzetnik. For the voice of a child came to him through one window, while he peered into another.

Auschwitz itself, he calls *Shivitti*. The LSD opened a window for him, as he described it. "I could never go back there," he explained, "but this was something like a window. I could look through it and see what I could never reach."

And so he looked.

He saw a factory into which infants were fed and from which smoke rose to a silent sky. As in many other factories, the machinery here was at work twenty-four hours a day. Like many other factories, this one had its own peculiar odor. For years he wondered what product was being produced there. And he finally realized what it was: it was the Bomb. Los Alamos did not produce that instrument of mass death, Yehiel insists. Auschwitz produced it. Hiroshima would have been impossible, unthinkable, without Auschwitz.

You see how Auschwitz expands the horizons of the imagination. The tale of Auschwitz, of the Six Million, becomes the tale of us all. The man who sent those children to the ovens is the man who can push the button. He *is* Man. We are all implicated, not only as possible victims but as potential executioners.

"One day," Yehiel related to me, "they were loading me onto a lorry with other men who were to be taken to the gas chamber. It was very early in the morning, before daylight. It was very cold too. There was a young man, an SS man, standing next to the truck in his coat. His hands were shoved into his pockets, and he yawned. I did not understand this. He did not want to be there. He would rather be in his warm bed. And we surely did not want to be there. Why, then, was it happening?

"And then the dark realization hit me: not only could he have been in my place, climbing on this truck destined for death, but I could have been in *his* place! I could have been the one sending this man to *his* death with a yawn! He was not a monster, but a man, cold and tired, as I was. How was this possible? How was it that we were both created in God's image? Who is this God?

"God created us in His image and gave us the imagination from which we in turn create Him. God did not make Auschwitz. Neither did a devil. It was man. Making Auschwitz, he made a new image of God. That new god is Nucleus!"

I found this image extremely revealing. Instead of peace, holiness, and wholeness—instead of *shalom*—we pursue and bow down to the epitome of fragmentation: the splitting of the atom. Matter is torn asunder, and with it so are we. We have become fragmentation incarnate, and that is why we are homeless. We who split the atom split families, homes, neighborhoods, countries, races, and, of course, ourselves. We do not know the people next door. We do not want to know them. And so we do not know ourselves.

The homeless? Hide them away, split them off. We do not want to hear about it. And so we are deaf even to the voice that summons us from our own souls. If, for a moment, the voice should break through the noise of this world that echoes the noise of the Bomb, then we run to psychologists who all too often plug our ears, cover our eyes, and spoon-feed us more opiate illusions. It is all connected.

Yehiel is right: the world did not end at Los Alamos. It ended at Auschwitz. That is where man undertook the murder of God. God is infinite in His goodness? Well, we can be infinite too—in our evil. No it wasn't the devil. It was man struggling to be God. We simply invent devils whenever we cannot bear to look upon ourselves. In *Shivitti* the novelist becomes a prophet whose prophecy is a revelation of the present.

The way Yehiel spoke of his first and last books made me wonder whether he would ever write another book. The first dealt with what had become of the image of man, the last with what had become of the image of God. The first was a history, the last a prophecy. The first was a testimony, the last a warning. What more is there to say? But there is always something more. The truth is always *more.*

And now this man—who has seen the undoing of God and man, who refuses recognition, who has wrestled, like Jacob, with the word and with life and with death, who is so gentle despite and because of it all, so kind, so intense, who needed to hug someone—now this man nurses the woman who spent a year forty-five years ago searching for him.

As I sat and listened to Yehiel, I could hear her coughing and at times choking in the next room. Yehiel could hear her too. He would excuse himself and go to her, her pain cutting through his face, his eyes, his soul. He had survived a world turned to ashes so that he could be at his wife's side and watch her ebb away. Was this why she had resurrected him from the dead? So that he could attend to her in her last days?

How is it possible? The more I see, the less I understand. What is this world? Who is its Creator? Why? Nothing fits. Speaking of it exhausts me. I write about it, reflect on it, and I feel my strength draining away a drop at a time. I am paralyzed and terrified. But we must speak. We must ask the questions.

His experience in Holland, the experience he describes in *Shivitti*, Yehiel told me, enabled him to see the Auschwitz that had eluded his consciousness. He found no answers in Holland, he said, but the therapy sessions at least helped him to ask the questions. What are the questions he is now asking as he watches his wife fade away, this woman famous in Israel for her love and devotion to people? It was she who saved him, she who gave him the key to the return of his soul.

He tells me about the memory of the child's cry as he was writing *Shivitti*, the cry that enabled him to keep his hold on life. And in the next room Eliyah cries out for him, like a child. I want to stay, to do something, say something, listen to him, be silent with him. My impotence is maddening, but I know I must leave him to his vigil and her to her passing. His eyes tell me it is time to go.

I rise from the sofa. Yehiel and I embrace. Holding him, I try to give him something to hold on to. I try to convey to him my love and my gratitude, my sorrow and my apology. I try to keep the scream in my throat from flooding the room. He is, after all, one of the few witnesses in life and to life who have made me into a witness and a messenger. How can I endure the debt?

"Write me," Yehiel asked. And, of course, I promised him I would. I am writing to him even now, writing for Eliyah.

Coming to Israel from Poland, I came from a place of

death to a place of life. And among the last faces I see in Israel is the face of a dying woman who tells me that she loves me. Everything is upside down. I look at her. I look at Yehiel. And I am overwhelmed by the weight of all I must atone for, by the distance I have yet to go in my endeavor to become a Jew. Each is responsible for all, and I more than the rest.

This is my last day in Israel. But it is not the last day of my encounter. Tomorrow I go to Amsterdam to see the place where a child hid for a time before she too was murdered. I have gone from one brink to another, each a preparation for the next, now plummeting, now soaring. At times the mystery draws nigh, at times it recedes, receding in its drawing nigh. Going to Auschwitz could not have happened for me without going to the man who emerged from that alien planet, who wrote the first testimony to be published.

I cannot know Auschwitz, but I can struggle to know the man. His eyes tell more than all the exhibits. Gazing into them, I can struggle to receive at an ever-increasing depth the message he transmits. I can struggle to come a bit closer to the barbed-wire fence, to return to myself, my family, my world with a greater capacity for response, embrace and affirmation. The embrace that Yehiel offered to me, the embrace that he needed from me, is one that must find its way into the embrace that I shall forever offer to my loved ones, to my friends, to my students.

I am sitting at a table in a sidewalk cafe. It is located at the intersection of Dizengoff and Nordau. Mothers are walking with their infants, some in their arms, others in baby carriages. I am amazed and gladdened at how many there are. Silently I say a *brachah* and give thanks to the Holy One, blessed be He. And it becomes all the more clear to me as to why I wear a *kipah*.

16 SIVAN 5751

Tel-Aviv, 29 May 1991

TODAY I GO TO Amsterdam, to the place where the child Anne Frank went into hiding. I have a friend who is doing some work on her. He told me he was trying to get at the "mystique of Anne Frank," and, indeed, there is something of a mystique about her. Why this child? Why is she the one to capture the imagination of the world? Traces of her soul are curled up in the margins and between the lines of her diary, where it addresses both itself and Another. Therefore it has the power to address the souls of us all.

Human imagination has made her into more than one more child fed into the death machine. She has become *the* child, the Eternal Child, placed into the category of symbol. And this means that through her diary and photographs not only does this child speak to us, but something of our own essence—or rather something beyond our essence—addresses us as well. Anne Frank becomes a means by which the veiled reveals itself, a portal through which the light and the darkness that threatens it may be glimpsed. Anne not only speaks to us—she chooses us. In her goodness, in her innocence, she announces to us that we are chosen by the Good before we make any other choices. She points to the evil that would swallow us up from within, and she embodies the Good that we have betrayed. She signifies the *hidden* that comes to light too late, always too late.

Faith does not mean that one day it will come, as Elie once told me; faith means that one day it was there. And that is what Anne Frank means. She tells us that the thing most dear in life is also most fragile, that there is something that must be nurtured, cared for, loved, and protected with our very lives, or else we shall lose everything that lends our lives any shred of meaning.

That is why this great and precious treasure is hidden: because it is so very fragile. In a way, Anne Frank is a symbol of the *Shechinah* herself. In those terrible times the meaning was drained from the word. The light fled the flame. And it was hiding in a small room on the upper floors of a house in Amsterdam, until one day it was devoured by…men.

I am on my way to bear witness to her empty room, by way of Auschwitz and Jerusalem—by way of what murdered her and was murdered within her. Certainly much of her significance is tied to what became of her. So I think the path to where she was hidden begins with the place where she was extinguished. As for her house—it is, after all, the Anne Frank *House* that one sees in Amsterdam—I believe it is so striking because it is a place of homelessness within a home and a home in the midst of homelessness.

Leaving Israel, I feel a great sadness, a very special sadness. It began to set in when I left Jerusalem. It seems as though I am returning to the world from a place that is both part of the world and beyond it. And yet I have the sensation of taking it all with me. For the holiness of the Holy City abides wherever there is a home and a family. And I am returning home. And that fills me with happiness.

◊

Amsterdam, 29 May 1991

I have just staggered out of Anne's room, just stumbled from her House. It is only a half mile or so from my hotel in downtown Amsterdam. I located the street called Prisengracht on a map and followed all the signifiers, until I came to the site where the House was located. Looking up from the map, I easily spotted the House from the long line of tourists that stretched out from the door and down the street. In front of it flowed a picturesque canal. Like a snake, the line wound its way into the House and through its rooms. Among the visitors were groups of schoolboys glancing at this, nodding at that, nudging each other in the ribs, with no apparent sense of where they were, no notion of the silence that the place demanded. Many of them were about Anne's age. Did they make the connection?

I paid the admission fee and followed more signs. The stairs going up to the hiding place were strikingly steep, more like a ladder than a flight of stairs. The steps led to a place suspended between heaven and earth, where the Frank family was veiled from the sun and removed from the soil. Not only was the light withheld from them, but a silence was imposed upon them. For during the day a business was in operation on the lower level of the building, so that they could not make a sound during business hours for fear that they might be discovered. They could neither run the tap water in their small, makeshift kitchen, nor flush the toilet. During business hours their business was silence.

The entrance to the passage that leads to the three small rooms where they lived was hidden behind a bookcase. This was astounding to me: the passageway to a hidden life led through the portal to what is hidden behind the books and the texts themselves. In order to get to the place where Anne tried to establish a semblance of dwelling, you have to penetrate a cabinet of texts. But, of course, the books were not enough to protect them. Books alone are never enough. He who knows only the study of the Torah, the Talmud tells us, knows nothing.

Above the bookcase was a map of the world, and once again it could not have been more overwhelming if it had been calculated by a brilliant stage director. The map was a sign of where they were *not*, a sign of the nonplace that was the hiding place. It seemed to say, "This is the world. This is where you no longer are. This is what no longer exists. Now you belong to an inside that has no outside." Yes, home belongs to the interior. But in order to become a home the interior must be one that can be externalized, one that can be taken into a community. The interior of the Anne Frank House was not of that sort.

On the other side of the case of words Anne wrote her diary, the text of her life, hidden beyond the wall like the life of humanity itself. As the Great Night reigned over the face of the earth, there burned in this attic the words of a child that contained a spark of light. The diary was a gift that her mother and father gave to her in 1942 for her thirteenth birthday. My daughter Miriam just turned thirteen. I could not help but picture her there, and as my imagination began to churn, my legs began to shake. No, not her, not here! Not this child! What are you doing?

For a long time I stood in Anne's room and looked at the pictures that she had cut from magazines and put up on her walls. Yes, I thought to myself, Miriam does that too. Most of the photos were of movie stars (yes, just like Miriam), but there was one picture that seemed out of place. It resembled one of the ancient Greek philosophers. Aristotle perhaps, although it was not the famous bust of him. It was an ancient image of ancient ideas on humanity and its meaning, ideas whose impotence was painfully demonstrated by the appearance of the Greek sage on the walls of that room.

The air in the room harbored an eerie presence. Its narrow space was filled with the spirit of that child's innocence and with the monstrous violation of that innocence. As I paced about its perimeter, my imagination soon became my enemy. Before me arose images of men—yes *men!*—wearing caps embossed with the death's head like a frontlet between the eyes, and the sign laid upon their arms: a swastika.

Their leather boots stomp up the stairs and through the passage no longer covered by the bookcase. The mother and father can hear the footsteps coming toward the hiding place, where now there is no place to hide. They go pale with fear for their children, Anne and Margot. Silent prayers burst from their lips as the men break into this dark sanctuary and lay cruel, dirty hands upon the little girl, her sad eyes peeled wide with terror. Her little face is contorted with screams, as she is brutally dragged down the steep stairs, taken into the street, and thrown into the van.

"Where are they taking me, Papa...?"

There I stood, these sounds reverberating in my ears. I have never wanted so desperately to rush home and put my arms around my children, around my wife. I leave Anne's room, and the faint noise of leather boots follows me. And I realize the obvious: the Anne Frank House is a haunted house.

Still following the signs, I proceeded to another room. It was filled with various editions of Anne's diary in dozens of languages. The familiar photo portrait on the cover of the published volumes of her diary is one of the simplest and yet most mysterious portrayals of innocence that I have ever seen. Looking at the diaries on display, I noticed that the two Soviet editions did not have her photograph on the cover but rather came with ugly drawings of the Jewish child that were loosely based on the photograph.

I say ugly, because these drawings looked as if they were calculated to make the Jew into something ugly. They reminded me of something out of an anti-Semitic propaganda poster made by the Nazis themselves. Instead of *The Diary of Anne Frank,* above the drawing they might have written *Der Ewige Jude.* Looking upon this insidious subtlety, I recalled that just days prior to his death Stalin was engineering plans to exterminate the Soviet Jews.

Among other exhibits in the House was the order for Anne's deportation from Westerbork to Auschwitz. Her name, along with the names of her parents and her sister Margot, appeared on a long list of names that included each person's date of birth. There were many children, many elderly. Children were old, Wiesel's words came to me, and old men were as helpless as children.

How did that little girl's mind grasp the sights she must have seen? She saw the killers kill. She saw the chimneys smoke. What horrible wound tore its way through her child's soul when she was torn from her mother and father? Her mother died there, in Auschwitz.

Only her father survived. He was liberated by the Russians after Anne and Margot had been sent to Bergen-Belsen, where they died of typhus in March 1945. Had she been able to hang on for just a few days longer, when the camp was freed, she might be sixty-two now, as she should be, a woman living out her life with memories of innocence and horror.

As it was, she died in innocence. As it is, she signifies the murder of innocence, and therefore the murder of God. The death of a man is horrible indeed, but it is just that, the death of a man. But the death of a child—the *murder* of a child—is the death of the Most High, the murder of the Most Dear. "Where is God now?" a character asks upon witnessing the execution of a child in Wiesel's

Night. And from Eliezer comes the terrible response: "Where is He? Here He is. He is hanging here on these gallows."

We turn to Anne Frank because in her life and in her death she signifies all that we long for, all that we are not, all that we never were and never shall be. The House contained many photographs of this child and her family. She is, in fact, the signifier of the family, the child without whom there can be no family and without whom, therefore, there can be no dwelling. Gazing upon her infinitely vulnerable face, I was overcome with a vain longing to take her into my arms and protect her, to tell her it's all right, I'm here, I won't let anything happen to you, just as I have done with my own little girls. Just as her father must have done.

His horror I cannot even contemplate.

"My daughter is dead. I am alive. And the universe is turned on end."

No longer does he ask, "How long, O Lord?" It is too late for that. He has lived past the end, lived too long. His heart continues to beat when it should have come to a stop, continues despite his longing for it to stop. He is the one to whom the task of memory has fallen. There is no survivor who is not thus bereaved.

"I alone am escaped to tell thee!"

And with his wounds, out of his wounds, he bears his message. I tried to draw close to him, but the closer I got, the more terrified I became.

And I tried to reach out to the child. I felt as though I had arrived not forty-seven years too late but forty-seven seconds, as if I had reached out to catch her and she had fallen just beyond my fingertips. My soul was flooded with excruciating guilt and maddening helplessness, with panicked frustration and nauseating remorse.

And a vision from Wiesel's *Ani Maamin* flashed through my mind. I saw a man running breathlessly, running fran-

tically and in vain, with a little girl in his arms. He knows
he cannot save her, and yet he runs with her, and she
clings to him, and she says to him, "I believe in you."

And suddenly I am that man, impotent and afraid.
What could I have done? What can I do? I do not know
why, but I know that it is my fault. I know that I am the one
responsible for this House and its haunting, for this child
and her searching eyes, for this father who must have gone
insane, despite all appearances.

Once again the loss of home comes back to me. Anne
and her family were forced to make a home in hiding and
in silence, forced to somehow dwell in a place that was not
suited to be a home. In her diary we have a sense of home
nonetheless, and that is what is so stunning: that someone,
a child—and perhaps only a child is capable of this—fosters a sense of home where by every right there should be
no such sense. It is a perfect instance of what Emmanuel
Levinas calls "an overflowing of meaning by nonsense."
Who can listen to this child's tale and not hear the voice of
God? Who can look into her eyes and not feel His eyes
looking into you? And who can stare into the face of her
father and not be crushed by His silence?

The Frank family abandoned its home in Germany to
escape the Nazi persecution. Once in Amsterdam, they
repeatedly sought passage to a new home in the United
States and were repeatedly refused (a point that helps me
to understand why Yehiel views English as the language of
those who turned their backs on the Jews). And so they
were forced into hiding and then into the death camps.
Give me your tired, your hungry, your persecuted. But not
your Jews.

But this child, this little girl—
No.
But—
No.

Anne's hiding place may have been the upper floors of

this house. But her home is the place that we have denied this Jewish child. And the other Jewish children of the world?

CNN reported yesterday that only 30% of Americans believe that the United States should ensure the security of Israel. They also reported that the policy of the White House reflects the majority view that the United States should have no particular stake in the security of Israel. Meanwhile we are seeing to the reconstruction of Kuwait and to the establishment of a neutral territory in Iraq for the Kurds. The White House and the Anne Frank House are more than just miles apart.

Anne, where are you, my child? Can you see the eyes of the Jewish children in Jerusalem, Tel-Aviv, and Haifa? Do you gaze back at them as they look upon the pages of your diary and into the innocence of your soul? Did you see the gas masks that covered their little faces?

In the Anne Frank House, from that house, Auschwitz reached out and suffocated the breath, the spirit, of life. In Jerusalem, from Jerusalem, other hands reach out and struggle to protect and preserve that spirit. The Israelis sent airplanes to rescue the Falashim of Israel. The Germans, with the help of millions of accomplices, sent trains to the Franks of Europe. Where do we stand? There is no middle ground. No neutrality. Neutrality is another word for indifference, and indifference is another word for death.

I wonder how Eliyah is doing. And Mrs. Gouri.

17 SIVAN 5751

Amsterdam, 30 May 1991

I **AM NEARING THE** completion of one pilgrimage and about to begin another. And it occurs to me that, in a way, each day can become a pilgrimage. The first words formed each morning on the lips of an observant Jew are "I give thanks before Thee," thanks for returning me not just to life but to a new life. The miracle of the morning is that each day we begin again and have the opportunity, by the grace of *HaShem*, to become something other, something more, than what we are. That is what distinguishes us from the animals. An animal is what it is. A human being is what he is yet to become. That is what makes a human being a pilgrim.

Soon, if it is God's will, I shall be on a flight for New York, then St. Louis, then Tulsa, then home. It should take about twenty-four hours. Right now I am so deluged with memories, so haunted with shadows, that I am not sure what to make of it all. Most of my time has been spent in silence. Certainly it is in silence that most of my encounters and collisions have taken place.

Yesterday, on the bus from Schipol into Amsterdam, I

spoke with a non-Jewish Russian who now lives in Tel-Aviv with his Jewish wife and two daughters. He told me that things are so hard for the Russians in Israel that about a third of them want to go back to the Soviet Union. I found this difficult to believe and very painful to hear. Can it be true? Is it possible that a Jew would prefer Russian anti-Semitism to a life, however difficult, in Erets Yisrael?

On this trip—perhaps only now, at the end of the trip—I have understood something more about a statement that I often make to my students: in all the world there is but a single place where a great treasure is hidden, and that place is the spot where you are standing. The difficulty in life lies in taking on the new eyes and the changed heart that enables us to see the treasure. I think that perhaps I have begun to receive those new eyes. Although it has been from a great distance, I have none-theless come face to face with the Angel of Death, the Angel of a Thousand Eyes, and he has left me with new eyes. And through those new eyes I am beginning to see life anew.

Treblinka, Majdanek, Auschwitz-Birkenau, the *Kotel,* Yad Vashem, the Gouris, the De-Nurs, the Anne Frank House—all of it has opened my eyes to a new and deeper part of my soul, and there I see, as if for the first time, the dearness and beauty of my wife Gerri, my daughters Miri-am and Rachel, my mother and father, my brothers Dan and Don, my friends, my students. This pilgrimage to the dwelling place of the Holy One and to the resting place of His Chosen has led me to these loved ones. I see now that on this journey they have been my destination all along, my wife and children above all, my wife especially. Before me I now see only their faces, drawn from the lines of all I have seen, all I have written.

❧

New York, 30 May 1991

Almost there. The flight to St. Louis has been delayed. I hope I won't miss my flight to Tulsa. I am so very weary but so very excited. My sole thought is to embrace my family and to make that embrace into a prayer of thanksgiving. Almost there.

Meanwhile I carry the stones in my pocket, along with the bit of Jewish earth from the grounds of Auschwitz-Birkenau. No doubt some of it is still stuck to the soles of my shoes. I have tracked it all over Jerusalem and Tel-Aviv, all through the Anne Frank House, and now I am tracking it home. Or is it tracking me? As I discovered in Poland, there is no round-trip ticket to Treblinka.

For once you have been there, you can never leave it behind. It latches onto you, like this red thread around my right hand, the hand that writes these lines. It is the slender, blood-red thread that a beggar tied to my wrist just outside the entrance to the Western Wall. Tying it to me, he tied me to more than I can imagine or merit. The responsibility is overwhelming. I pray that I may have the strength and the character to live up to it. I entered those places, those times. And now they have entered me, entered with my return home. Return...almost there...

I just spoke to Gerri on the phone to tell her about the delays in the flights leaving New York. As ever—no, more than ever—her voice was a ray of light that penetrated into my heart. My lips moved with a silent prayer of gratitude when she told me that my little girls are fine and that they would all meet me tonight at the Tulsa airport. I feel so happy, so blessed, that it rather scares me.

In a way, I also feel horribly guilty for knowing a happiness that the Six Million never had a chance to know, that most of the world can never know. It is a bliss that is definitively and inextricably connected to a profound Jewishness that has ignited within me. I know that this something inside is Jewish, because it is marked by a profound gratitude and an equally profound responsibility. Maybe these two words signify the same state of being, like words such as *love, joy, faith, righteousness, spirit*. Like the word *Jew*.

Gerri told me that the *New York Times* mentioned Gouri's involvement with the airlift of the Falashim. That explains why I did not hear from him on that Friday in Jerusalem. What I ever did to merit knowing him, Eliyah, Yehiel, Liat, all of Israel, I shall never know. But I shall be forever thankful.

If ever I should forget thee, O Jerusalem: O Auschwitz…!

◊

St. Louis, 30 May 1991

The delay in New York caused me to miss the last flight from St. Louis to Tulsa. It was not God's will that I should sleep in my bed tonight. Gerri was not thrilled with the news, but at least I am closer to home than I was twenty-four hours ago. So here I am, sitting alone once again in a hotel room. It was not yet time for my journey to end. The silence needed a little more space, a little more time. Perhaps this journal needed just a few more lines. Tomorrow the last leg, the last lines.

18 SIVAN 5751

IT WAS NOT THE WILL of the Holy One, blessed be He, that I should arrive home yesterday, but (God willing) I shall arrive home today, Erev Shabbat. It seems altogether fitting that the first evening I spend at home with my family should be the evening of the Sabbath. I shall be reunited with my family at a time when life is itself once again made whole. Yes, it is fitting.

Each Sabbath I spent abroad—the first in Warsaw, the second in Jerusalem—had a very deep significance for me. And the significance of those two Sabbaths spent abroad will pour into the meaning of the Sabbath of my return. In Warsaw and in Jerusalem I suspended the writing of these notes in remembrance and observance of the Sabbath. Now it seems both fitting and wise that this journal come to a close with my homecoming for the Sabbath. The Sabbath is itself a time of return. As the Eternal returns to time, so does the human being return to the Place, to the *Makom*, that is God.

These days that I have passed in other lands have been about home and homelessness, history and eternity, life and death, memory and exile. Bringing me home on this day, after all those days on the other shore, God seems to be offering me a glimpse of the holiness that until now I had only intimated, as though He were allowing me to see some small part of the Jewish being that made me a proselyte, the being that belongs to the Sabbath. The Midrash tells us that in the Sabbath we have a portion of the World to Come. Perhaps on this Sabbath, as I greet in my bride the Sabbath Bride, I may rejoice in some small portion of the Jew that I strive to become.

I think I see more clearly now what Heschel meant when he said that what we are lies in what the Sabbath means to us. If that is true—since that is true—what we are lies in our endeavor to return, in the *teshuvah* we seek each day in the utterance of the Prayer and in the embrace of our loved ones. And this means that what we are lies in what we are *not yet*, in what we are in the process of becoming, in the path we have taken up. This journey and this journal leading from Auschwitz to Jerusalem have entailed a process of transformation: what was has been made into a new horizon of the *yet-to-be*. And that transformation entails a transformation of the soul, a becoming more Jewish within my soul.

When what has been is made into the womb of the yet-to-be, presence happens. And this brings me back to the Sabbath, that portal through which the *Shechinah*, God's Indwelling Presence, returns to our lives and thus returns us to life by instilling us with presence. On the Sabbath we are released from the preoccupations of *melachah*, from the endless effort to manipulate time and space, that removes us from ourselves and from one another. On the Sabbath we are free to be where we are.

And so what must I now do with the things that I have looked upon and that have looked into me? How do I now complete this pilgrimage, this transfiguration, that has unfolded from Auschwitz to Jerusalem?

I think the answer lies in this: All that I have encountered, the little that I have understood, must be poured into the depth of my embrace of my wife and children, of my family and friends, of my students. The message is an ancient one, often repeated. But when it comes to us through the ashes of Majdanek and the stones of the *Kotel*, when it passes through these places and emanates from these depths, it assumes a greater capacity to speak what cannot be spoken, to convey what cannot be conveyed, and to affirm what is beyond the scope of affirmation.

I have just heard the boarding call, just heard the call. I am homeward bound, blessed be the Holy One.

Epilogue

Exactly THREE MONTHS have gone by since my return home. I just made a long-distance call to Eliyah. She is still with us, thanks be to God, and is doing as well as can be expected. Even as she is dying, in fact, I have known very few who were so alive.

"Think of Yehiel and me," she said, "as the angels Michael and Gabriel who are forever with you."

And I do so think of them. Indeed, when I am in their presence, I have the feeling of being in the presence of angels. I sense them with me even now, even here, between the lines and along the margins of these pages. Or are they the ones, these angels, who are reading over my shoulder?

But angels sometimes put disturbing questions to us and wrestle with us, as the angel wrestled with Jacob. Their very presence summons us to reckoning.

As I spoke with Eliyah today, I was reminded that the outcome of a pilgrimage is always an increase in the depths of one's responsibility. More than ever, the first question God put to the first man comes forth from the face of everyone I meet: Where are you? And with it, like a shadow, comes the question that God put to the first son of the first man: Where is your brother? The two, of course, are of a piece. If I cannot answer for my brother, then I cannot be either who I am or where I am. My presence before the Holy One is a presence before my fellow human being.

Where, then, is my brother? I look back over these pages and I see that he is there, in the handful of ashes that stretch from Auschwitz to Jerusalem. And now they stretch into my home as well. Stepping before the ashes, I must answer to all and for the sake of all. Having made the pilgrimage, I must make it again. And in this repetition, in this return, lies my one hope of ever declaring, "Here I am, the Jew Avraham David ben Avraham!"

Index